BEATIFIC VERITIES

"My words shall not pass away"
Jesus

Wallace Bassett, D. D.

THE WESTERN BAPTIST PUBLISHING COMPANY
Kansas City, Mo.
1917

Library 8407
Cliff Temple Baptist Church
Dallas, Texas

Copyright © 2008 by Wallace Bassett Estate
Published by arrangement with
Advanced Concept Design

Library of Congress Control Number
to be assigned
International Standard Book Number
ISBN 13: 978-0-9799723-8-6
All rights reserved.
No part of this book may be used or reproduced in any manner whatsoever, without written permission, except in the case of brief quotations embodied in critical articles and reviews, as provided by U.S. Copyright Law.

For information, address
rseibert@advancedconceptdesign.com
axlerod@peoplepc.com

First paperback printing June 2008
Printed in the United States of America

Publisher's Word

When I was a young man, in the late 1960's, and the world around me was filled with anger and turmoil, one lone voice stood out in my surroundings, crying like a prophet of old, and surrounded by naysayers on all sides, Wallace Bassett was a beacon.

*He alone stood for a shining liberality, that blew through the halls of our community like a breath of fresh air. I owe him a great deal, and yet I never had the privilege of having heard him speak. I had only the words of others said against him. I thought that what I heard was not to his shame but his credit, and I thought that someday I should try to make a biography of him. This remains for a future work, but **Beatific Verities** is again* available in print for those who have ears.

Ray Seibert
Advanced Concept Design
June 2008

Contents

Chapter I. 2
The Tides of Providence As They Ebb and Flow 2
Chapter II 8
The Beatific Verity On Poverty Of Spirit 8
Chapter III 16
The Beatific Verity On Mourning 16
Chapter IV 23
The Beatific Verity On Meekness. 23
Chapter V 30
The Beatific Verity On Spiritual Dissatisfaction 30
Chapter VI 37
The Beatific Verity On The Merciful. 37
Chapter VII 45
The Beatific Verity On The Pure In Heart. 45
Chapter VIII 53
The Beatific Verity On The Peacemakers. 53
The Beatific Verity On The Persecuted For Righteousness' Sake. 61
Chapter X 68
The Beatific Verity On True Manhood. 68
Chapter XI 76
The Beatific Verity On Motherhood. 76

Chapter XII 84

The Beatific Verity On Childhood. 84

Chapter XIII 92

The Beatific Verity On The Forgiven. 92

Chapter XIV. 99

The Beatific Verity On The Religious Nation...................99

Chapter XV..106

The Beatific Verity On The Approved. 106

Chapter XVI. 113

The Beatific Verity On Faith In The Unseen Christ.......113

Chapter XVII. 120

The Beatific Verity On Liberality. 120

Chapter XVIII 126

The Beatific Verity On Not Being Offended In Christ. ..126

Chapter XIX 132

The Beatific Verity On The Dead In The Lord. 132

Introduction

The Beatitudes-when will they lose their charm? Never, so long as hungry and weary and sorely tried human hearts yearn for the hidden manna of future promise and present comfort, and so long as men's souls have that in them which can not be satisfied with the standards and ideals which are dominant in the Christless "world" around us. For it is as comfort and as challenge that these great words of Jesus come; challenge to nobler things, comfort while we are seeking them.

We welcome, therefore, every fresh presentation of these celestial assurances and celestial ideals, so elementary among the principals of the Kingdom of Heaven, and yet so far beyond the present attainment of society, and even of the churches; in fact, their fulfillment in any single life, except one, has yet been only partially accomplished. If, as we see to be the fact, the Beatitudes are the A B C of the Kingdom, what must be the "postgraduate course" of God's great institution? But it shall be ours to be graduated in, never graduated from, that blessed instruction. And the Beatitudes themselves assure us that these "Beatific Verities" shall all some time exhibit in us their full power of character and blessing.

"Blessed are they that hunger and thirst after righteousness: for they shall be filled"

To these gathered Beatitudes of the Master in Matthew Five, Dr. Bassett has added other promises of blessing from the Testaments, Old and New, chiefly single sayings of the Master, covering a wide range, and has given us these brief, bright, popular expositions, sufficiently scholarly, but with the breezy breath of the open religious platform in them, and the vitality of the modern life. They are the actual "homilies" of a living Twentieth Century preacher to a living Twentieth Century people.

The themes taken from these great verses are high, attractive, and eminently worth while. Who would not be profited by considering " The Christian Fundamental," "Smiling Through Tears," "Where Heaven Touches Earth," The Discipline of Discontent," "That Blessed Mother," and topics like that?

Dr. Bassett, whom I count myself happy in reckoning as one of my pupils in the comfortably, but not too distant past, has done his work well. Imaginative insight, sympathy with the best, and for the neediest, in our modern life, is here, with clear unfolding, abundant illustration, and stirring, tender, inspiring expression. Under his leadership these "Beatific Verities" will bring a new vision to many, a new grip on the old truths to many more, and help to all who read.

PHILLIP WENDELL CRANNELL,
President Kansas City Theological Seminary.

Introduction

I have just finished reading the manuscript of Rev. Wallace Bassett on Beatific Verities. It was a joy to my soul from beginning to end. Dr. Bassett is the aggressive pastor of the First Baptist Church of Amarillo, Tex., an able preacher, scholarly in tastes, a clear thinker and a prodigious reader of various kinds of literature. In this monograph the author discusses, in sermonic style, the beatitudes of Jesus, in the Sermon on the Mount and those collected elsewhere by the New Testament writers, and of the Psalms. He closes with the beatitude pronounced by the risen Christ upon the dead in the Lord. The homiletic element is prominent in this superb series of discussions, but beneath the sermonic appeal is seen the correct interpretation of each beatitude in its original setting. The author also shows that he is familiar with the conclusions of modern scientists on many significant physical, social and ethical problems. The book is virile and thoughtful, and will make a commanding appeal to thinking men and business men. The analysis of meekness in Chapter IV., the crowning of stalwart manhood in Chapter X., and the eulogies on mercy, motherhood, and childhood in Chapters VI.,XI., and XII., respectively, set forth some universal verities of the moral universe as interpreted by Jesus and will find a welcome response in the hearts of all classes of people. These pages exalt Jesus as superior to his own age and the greatest ethical and religious thinker of any age. This little book will prove a spiritual and intellectual tonic to anyone who reads it with open mind and heart. I take great pleasure in introducing this young author to the reading public.

C.B.WILLIAMS,

Dean and professor, Southwestern Baptist Theological Seminary, Fort Worth, Texas

Foreword

At the time these sermons were first preached in a series to the First Baptist Church, Amarillo, the author had no idea of having them published. The decision to have them published was reached because of four things- the requests of many who heard them-a general lack of literature along this line, discovered at the time of their preparation- the changes through which the world is now passing and the necessity for something abiding in belief and in Christian activity- and the request from the publishers which came unexpectedly and unsought at the very time these other thoughts were most forcefully being brought home to the mind.

We ask our readers to be kind enough to consider the fact that there addresses were first prepared to be delivered as sermons. While we have tried to be more or less true to the rules of exegesis and the laws of historical study, reading every passage in the original and studying it in the light of the historical situation, yet this book was written for the average churchgoer who knows nothing about exegesis and little about historical interpretation.

Our aim is to bring us more to the ideas as given us by Jesus, and to cause us to more unhesitatingly adopt his platform. With this prayer, we send forth our book.

W.B.

Things Which Abide.

Heaven and earth shall pass away, but my words shall not pass away (Matt. 24:35)

Chapter I.

The Tides of Providence As They Ebb and Flow.

While walking down the side street of a village, I chanced to see the place where a house once stood. All that remained of this house was a huge chimney. Alone and lonesome-like this chimney stands in a sea of ashes and charred lumber. As I walked through a wood, my thirst compelled me to bend over a laughing stream to drink. As I drank, I noticed the solid rock bottom, over which the stream had run "for nobody knows how long." In the road of the stream over the rock, I noticed high places that the flow of the stream had not leveled to the surface of the rock.

This world of ours has passed through many fires of upheaval and revolutionary formation. Each one of these fires represents a thousand years put into a single day. Much goes before these blazes, and from the ashes no more similar buildings can phoenix-like arise. This old world has passed through centuries on evolutionary progress and the "wear and tear" of time has gradually smoothed many things. These things are gone to the land "from whose bourne no traveler returns." But after the smoke of the fire is gone, we see part of the house still standing. It was evidently built of fireproof material. This part of the house was put into the fire before it was put into the house. After the stream had passed for years over the surface of the rock, some of the surface refused to be leveled by the continued kissing of the flowing water. It was more durable material.

Our present age is one of blow pipe and test tube. Everything is put to the test. Many things thus tested are going the way of all the earth. There are some things that stand the storm and stress of time. As the fires of revolution crack and blaze, and as the waters of evolution smoothly and quietly run, let us look at the durable things left to us. Let us examine the things unchanged and unchanging.

There is no phase of our life that will be able to slip by the man who asks questions, and no part of our being that will be exempt from the acid test.

The lives of governments are now being subjected to the most demanding examination in the history of the world. In many instances disorganization and destruction are bound to follow. In the past, governments have arisen and fallen "like bubbles on the water." In the not-far-distant future they are to sink like the waters of Niagara, amid great noise, but not to come up again. The tides of Providence are not to be resisted. No man can turn back the hands on God's clock. The European struggle is not a accident, and the varied results of it on the world will be eternal in significance.

The social life, as we live it today, will also be subjected to this trial. The fact that it is organized and complex does not mean it will pass through no more changes. All social ideas, attitudes, customs and practices must weigh enough or be thrown out of the scales.

The life as we live it in the business world will be questioned. There will be two questions asked men of business: the one will be how they accumulated their money, and the other, how they spend it. These two questions will have to be answered acceptably, or the man of business will not be permitted to pass. Nor will the public take "none of your business" for an answer. It has a right to know these two things, and to act on the ground of the knowledge received.

This examination of time also extends to the realm of faith and to the life of religion. Theologies born to meet certain conditions in certain ages are changing eternally. When newer conditions arise we may expect and prepare for more changes, for they are sure to come. The man with questions, who comes from laboratories, will not accept man-made theories, age-made traditions, or church-made rules and regulations. He is going to demand in the future, more than he has in the past, fruits and facts. Can our religious ideas meet this acid test? Needless to say to any one acquainted with facts, that many of the ideas once held and practiced are gone never to return, and that the world is richer since their going. Furthermore, it can be seen by any one with eyes that many more are going. "Wood, hay and stubble" will not stay in the fire unchanged.

* * * * * * * * *

Now that we must have a platform on which to stand is seen and recognized by writers in both the secular and religious press, and voiced from pulpit and platform with unction and power. What principles will abide? Whose philosophy is time-proof and secure in both the evolutions and revolutions of life?

There are two that rush to our aid. The one is the world and the other is Christ. The world's philosophy finds voice through Nietzsche. The voice is that of the natural man, which, of course, is the speech; of selfishness. This voice depreciates the; value of humanity and underestimates the price of a soul. When it speaks through the lips of Napoleon, it says, "To have an omelet we must break a few eggs." It says if a man harm you, in return you must harm him. It says, "Do the other fellow as he might do you; only you do him first." It talks of revenge, of iron of might and of taking care of one's own self and interests. Now these thoughts of the world were not born with the man who so forcefully spoke them. They are as old as sin and were the fundamental principles of the law of the jungle. Our forebears lived by them when they were wearing for clothing the skins of wild animals and drinking blood from the skulls of enemies. The remedy proposed by the world has made nothing permanent that has accepted it. We must turn to the second help that is offered and see if it will do as it claims.

Christ's words will not pass away, though heaven and earth may. In all the centuries gone, the only ideas not outlived have been his ideas. They are eternal because they can be incarnated into characters and lives; and in accepting them, the recipients are always elevated. His principles of life will make a nation, a home, an organization, or an individual great and abiding. Yuan Shi Kai is reported to have said to Dr. H. H. Lowry, "Only Christian ethics can save China." I do not know whether he said it or not, but he could have said it with truthfulness. He could have added further that this is the only salvation for England, Russia, Germany or America. Christ brings to a nation the sense of the worth of a human being, not because he is a king, or a man with brass buttons, but because he is a man. "Kind hearts are more than coronets" in his sight. Pure democracy was born from the travail of Christian progress, and only pure democracy can hope to be the final government. Some things we have been calling Christian must go, but worthwhile things in all realms will stay. A great man recently said, "Nothing that does not make for a truer social life for mankind, and for the highest of our spiritual ideals, will be allowed to call itself Christian any longer."

The beatitudes of Jesus, and the other beatific expressions, give voice to verities the writer firmly believes to be fundamental and abiding. He thinks these truths will be voiced and lived
> "When the sun grows cold,
> And the stars are old,
> And the leaves of the judgment book unfold"

We do not say that these verities are all-inclusive, and that all other ideas shall cease; but these verities express our present message to the world. These, it seems to us, are part of the unchanging things of Jesus and the Gospel and they shall be here after the tides of Providence have ebbed and flowed.

The Christian Fundamental.

Blessed are the poor in spirit: for theirs is the kingdom of heaven (Matt. 5:3)

Chapter II

The Beatific Verity On Poverty Of Spirit

The Sermon on the Mount occupies the same place in the teaching of our Savior that the Mosaic Law occupies in the Old Testament teachings. This being true, we may add that the Beatitudes occupy the same place with reference to the Sermon on the Mount that the Ten Commandments occupy with reference to the Mosaic Law. There is much thought expressed in few words in this series of remarkable statements. Not only do we see every principle expressed in these Beatitudes which is amplified in the following Sermon on the Mount, but he never gives voice to a parable, or performs a miracle, or does an act, or speaks a word which has not been anticipated in these remarkable statements. 'These sentences have gripped the thought of the world. They are quoted more than any other statements in the whole Bible, but they are not preached from as frequently as they should be. Coleridge says of them, "The Beatitudes are the grandest expression of thought in the literature of the world."

Now, every one of these statements contradicts the existing standards of the time, and if followed out would have completely revolutionized existing social and political conditions. They seem mild and negative, and some superficial students of them have gained enough courage to so express themselves. But they have not read in them the meaning of Christ as he intended it. Every expression comes from a brave heart and opposes forces as they then existed If carried out today in our dealings with one another, they will work wonderful changes. This message to the world is the only hope it had then or has now. They need a national acceptance as well as an individual one. Nations and individuals have grown toward civilization as they grew away from brute force toward the standards of Christ.

There are eight of these statements in the Sermon spoken on the side of the mountain. These eight statements express eight characteristics as lived and possessed by the person who has the Christ character in the world. They are not dealing with eight different persons, but one ideal person, according to the standards of Jesus. These eight characteristics are as admirable now as ever before.

Of these eight separate statements, one is fundamental and one is a conclusion. Their arrangement is not accidental. The first one gives the foundation on which all Christian character is built. The last one speaks of the relation of such a character to environment. Now all the beatitudes, except these two, speak of results which are to come in the future, but these two refer to results as they are now possessed-"Theirs is the kingdom of heaven."

The fundamental beatitude is "Blessed are the poor in spirit: for theirs is the kingdom of heaven." Poverty of spirit is the trait of the Christian which must precede all Christian growth and development of character. This is an expression of an attitude toward God, self and the world. It is a means toward an end, not an end in itself. The Stoics made it an end, and as a result they depreciated themselves enough to consider the taking of their own lives a virtue. But the noblest and most elevating ideals come from this trait of character, if we see it as a means toward an end.

What do we mean by poverty of spirit? It does not mean poverty of purse. It seems to me that certain expositors have gloriously missed the real meaning of our Christ when they have thus interpreted this text. We know many persons who are not poor in purse, but who are indeed and in truth poor in spirit. Abraham was known for his poverty of spirit, but he was not poor in purse. On the other hand some of the most independent, haughty persons of the world now, and in the past, have been those who were quite poor of purse. The real meaning of it is to be a beggar in spirit. To know we have spiritual needs and to express these spiritual needs, is spiritual poverty. It means not to be self-sufficient in our lives, but to be, on the other hand, cognizant of imperative need from God of both power and help.

Christ is the greatest example the world has ever had in this admirable trait of character. There is a contrast brought out here in the beginning of this sermon and in Isa. 53rd Chapter, "He opened his mouth and taught them saying," and, "as a sheep before her shearers is dumb, so he openeth not his mouth." On both of these occasions, the one when he spoke and the one when he was silent, he expressed this same message, and the fundamental teaching of this message is "Blessed are the poor in spirit." The world had been talking about what Jesus would say when he came and opened his mouth. The woman at the well said, "When the Messiah comes he will tell us much we do not know." But the persons who had watched his life knew what he was to say, for he only said what he had already lived.

This can be seen rather forcefully in Matthew's arrangement of the Sermon in its relation to the temptations. The Sermon is given by Matthew right after the temptations in the wilderness. There Satan had tried to get him to incarnate the opposite principle into his Messianic character. Every temptation which came to him was prefaced with the statement "If thou be the Son of God." This was asking him to maintain his rights and proceed in ;his life on his prerogatives of Sonship to God. Make stones into bread, fall down from the top of the pinnacle of the temple, gain control of material kingdoms, were the three offers made to the Savior. Every one of them, if yielded to would have caused Jesus not to keep in his work the poverty of spirit he advised his disciples to possess. He answered every temptation with a verse of Old Testament scripture; but he could have answered each one with the words Matthew places soon after the temptation, "Blessed are the poor in spirit: for theirs is the kingdom of heaven."

Now our Christ not only incarnated this fundamental principle into his life, but he also taught his disciples to become possessors of the same spirit. He, in his training of the twelve, gave them more lessons urging a poor spirit and insisting on their not being ambitious, than on any other subject. On one occasion when they were debating as to which one was to be chief among them, he called a little child to him and placed him in the midst and told his disciples to become like the child or they should not enter the kingdom, much less be great in it. Entrance into the kingdom was conditioned on the same thing that growth in it is conditioned on, and that is poverty of spirit. He, in this instance of the little child, said, by a beautiful deed, the same thing to which he gave voice by a wise word, when he said, "Blessed are the poor in spirit" for theirs is the kingdom of heaven."

There are many other places where Christ amplified by parable and deed this great statement of his. The prodigal son came home when he became poor in spirit. The Syro-Phoenician woman received what she desired when she became poor in spirit.

Perhaps the one outstanding parable illustrating this principle, is that of the Pharisee and publican. The Pharisee was the best man and also the worst man in the country. He was the best man morally, in that he was outwardly correct. He was the worst man, in that he was not poor in spirit, and therefore could not be better. No man is a good as he ought to be, who is as good as he wants to be. Now the publican was the worst man and also the best man in the country. He was the worst man from the moral view point. He was a sinner of the out-and-out kind. He associated with only such as were sinners. He was a national outcast, who was an extortioner and a cheat. He had no patriotism, for he was willing to collect taxes for the hated Romans. No self-respecting Jew would be guilty of such. But while he was the worst man, he was also the best, not morally, but by possessing a possibility of growth. He was poor in spirit. No man is as bad as he can be, who is not as good as he wants to be. Because of his poverty of spirit he was commended by our Lord.

Our Savior here is trying to put first things first. He is dealing with being and not with doing. He knows if he can get us to be what he wants us to be, we will do the right thing. He is more concerned with the nature of the tree in this instance than he is with the fruit of the tree. He knows if we are poor in spirit we will be true in our relations to our fellow men.

Now this beatitude, like all the other, forms a contrast. All of them a paradoxes. "Poor in spirit" is set over against "Theirs is the kingdom of heaven." We think of the kingdoms as great possessions. But according to his statement, the person who is really poor in attitudes is to be really rich in realities. It says theirs "is the kingdom," no "will be." It puts the man in possession of great wealth at the same time he is in possession of great poverty.

Dan Crawford wrote from the long grasses of Central Africa, "Have you ever noticed the first occurrence of the phrase, Son of man, and compared it with its last usage? The first time, it refers to the Son of Man who 'hath not where to lay his head.' The last time in the Bible usage is, 'the Son of Man, having on his head a golden crown.'" This is a beautiful conception which brings out the principle voiced in our text.

There are three New Testament uses of the term, "kingdom of heaven." All three of these uses can be applied to this verse, because poverty of spirit is the cause of our receiving them all. We speak of the kingdom of God as being within us. This is the meaning of the passage that tells us it is not eating and drinking, but righteousness, peace, and joy in the Holy Ghost. To have the kingdom of heaven in your heart, you must be poor in spirit. We sometimes speak of the kingdom of heaven from the militant viewpoint. In this sense we use the term to designate an aggressive body composed of all the Christians on the earth. All who recognize the kingship of Jesus are included in the kingdom in this sense. Then we use it in the eschatologicial sense. We, of course, mean here, the kingdom we shall have after death.

Now we must be possessors of poverty of spirit, or we shall never enter the kingdom in any sense whatever. "If we confess our sins, he is faithful and just to forgive us our sins, and to cleanse us from all unrighteousness." To confess, we must feel the beggarly element in our souls. Frederick the Great wrote to the Senate, "I have just lost a great battle and it is entirely my fault." Goldsmith said, "This confession displayed more greatness than all his victories." Some one has said that the three hardest words to pronounce in the English language are, "I was mistaken." Perhaps this is true, but no three words show the proper spirit better than these three. To begin the Christ life, we must begin where he began his beatitudes, and that is at the bottom.

> *"Nothing in my hand I bring,*
> *Simply to thy cross I cling."*

Smiling Through Tears.
Blessed are they that mourn: for they shall be comforted (Matt. 5:4)

Chapter III

The Beatific Verity On Mourning

In Matthew 5:4 Jesus gives us his Beatific Verity on Mourning. This is necessary if his is to be a universal message, for one of the chief concerns of life is sorrow. There are three universal languages. Watch a company of people whose language you do not speak, and whose language you do not understand, and you can see the three. When they become amused at anything, they all laugh. You can understand this without an interpreter. When they are vexed, or abused, they become angry, and you can understand this language also, without an interpreter. Then when they are sad, or when there is sorrow or affliction, they mourn. These three languages need no one to tell us their meaning, for they are universal. We all have an understanding of mirth, anger and sorrow.

"Your lot is the common lot of all;
Into each life some rain must fall-
Some days must be dark and dreary."

Sorrow is a universal thing, because that which causes sorrow and mourning is universal. Perhaps we could say there are four causes of grief in the world-pain, sympathy, sorrow and sin. These are universal, and so are the results of them. Earliest man, when he was discovered, was a weeping animal. The earliest portrayals of human beings present them to us as capable of grief and mourning.

Now these things being true, it must follow that any religion that hopes to receive a universal following, after the tides of Providence have ebbed and flowed, must have a positive message for those who mourn. The ancient heathen religions did not have a message for those who mourn. The ancient heathen religions did not have a message for the sad and sorrowing, and as a result the world has shown a willingness to discard them. They considered it a sigh of weakness to weep, and did not hesitate to so express themselves. But to simply tell a mourning one it is weakness to weep, will not remove the cause or alter the purpose in the least. The First Century Romans must be classed with all the heathen religions of the past. The Roman had no time for, or sympathy with, any who were in sorrow. Their work in the world was to cause sorrow, not to bring help in it. Theirs was a military age, like some would make this age. No military age expressed sympathy for sorrow. So they were in the world, as far as sorrow was concerned, as though they were not.

Modern heathenism, Christian Science, denies the very existence of the things which cause grief. But this does not touch the cause in the least. It rather sounds the death knell of Christian Science, for the world wants, and will have, a religion which will help them in their sorrows. When cholera broke out in India, the British Medical Association sent over leading physicians and the necessary equipment to relieve the suffering. They went to one Brahman priest and showed him the germs under a microscope, and asked him for his help. Why, what was his help? Simply to break the instrument. Now that did not influence the disease germs in the water in the least. So, shutting our eyes to the anguish and sorrow and sin of the world does not remove them. This is like the ostrich in its habits of hiding.

Christ recognized grief as being here. He came to relieve it and help to make people happy. In this he was only fulfilling the prophets. They spoke of his coming as a time when the days of mourning should be ended. It tells us of a time when the desert shall rejoice and blossom as a rose. He was a man of sorrows and acquainted with grief, that he might bear our griefs and carry our sorrows. After he came he fulfilled all these prophecies with respect to himself. When John the Baptist became doubtful as to his being the Christ, and sent his messengers to find out new evidence, Jesus referred to his healing the sick and raising the dead. If you carefully read over this list of things Christ mentioned here that he was doing, you will see that every one of them was a grief-relieving work.

We can, by looking out on life, see the general possibility of getting gladness from sadness and joy from mourning. It is far better to have mourned and been comforted than never to have mourned at all. We who mourn in poverty of spirit, are more godly as a result. This of course, is the second beatitude, and should be considered in its relation to the first. But considering the poverty of spirit to precede, then mourning is a spiritual discipline. The graduation in nature is determined by ability to suffer. The lowest animals are the ones that suffer least. This same principle can be applied to human beings, for the crudest and rudest human beings are those who are least capable of suffering.

It is in one sense a price of victory. Steel is simply iron which has gone through the testing fire. The statue is but rough marble, plus the mallet and chisel. A house is a tree, plus saws, planes, axes and hammers. Fierce heat and carbon will produce the diamond. You have to darken the cage of the nightingale in the day time to make it sing. The kernel of the nut is sweetened by the biting frosts of autumn. "The rainbow! See how fair a thing God hath built up from tears." Some one said that if an astronomer would secure some telescope which could aid him in seeing the remote confines of a tear, he could thus be able to see to heaven's remotest bounds. Moses, when a babe, depended on a tear on a chubby cheek to win for him a happy home and to turn the providences of God for a whole nation. "He that goeth forth and weepeth, bearing precious seed, shall doubtless come again with rejoicing, bringing he sheaves with him."

Our Savior came into direct touch with tears and removed them. In doing this he deals with the causes of grief. One way he has of dealing with grief is to lift pain or sorrow from the realms of the accidental into the realms of the purposeful. He causes us to see it as a part of a whole. A man was carving a small part of a beautiful flower leaf on a large rock. He was asked by a passer-by what he was doing, and his answer was, "following a blue print." His work was a drudgery, until one day he saw that little part of the leaf he had carved was fitted into a great flower and made into a large building. Seeing it in it relation to the other parts, he could understand the beauty of it all. So with our pains and troubles: Christ raises them into the realm of purpose, and we are made to see them in their relation to other things. Mr. Beecher illustrates this beautifully: he speaks of going through an organ factory and hearing the organ makers tune their pipes. There is no harmony, and every sound is a displeasing one, but when all these pipes are tuned and put together, they make a grand organ, which will respond to a master in a wonderful manner. The difference between grief and laughter is that one is discord and the other is harmony. That is why we do not like to hear crying, and always rejoice to hear laughter. But Jesus lifts the discord of grief into tune and puts the whole system together.

Not only does Jesus make us see the purpose of it all, but he also raises grief into the realm of the vicarious.

The reason Jesus endured the cross was because he was dying for someone else. We can go through much suffering in a heroic manner when we are made to see that by so doing we are serving and helping others. Paul speaks of his stripes and imprisonment, but also tells us how he is rejoicing in it all. His reason for this comfort is that these things have resulted in the furtherance of the Gospel.

Jesus also tries to raise it into the realm of self-discipline. It is by pulling the string that the kite goes higher. Charles Edward Locke repeats an often repeated story of a violin maker, who was asked to make a violin for a great musician, which he did after weary months of work. When the violinist drew the bow over the strings, the sounds were displeasing to him, and he smashed the instrument to pieces on the floor and turned and walked from the house. Later the violin maker asked the musician to come to see him and try another instrument which he did, and liked the violin very much. He was informed that this was the same instrument which he had smashed some time before. It took the smashing to give it the necessary tones. Jenny Lind was singing on one occasion, when the German musician, Goldschmidt, heard her. He said he could detect a little harshness in her tones, and if he could marry her and break her heart, this harshness would not be. This he later did, and persons who heard her said that the bit of harshness had left her voice. George Matheson's beautiful hymn, "Oh Love That Will Not Let Me Go," was born in a great sorrow.

Now the last cause of grief, which is sin, Jesus removes altogether. He forgives the sin and brings the sinning soul into right relations with God. At the same time, he engenders a hatred toward sin.

None of these things can be accomplished unless our mourning is preceded by a poverty of spirit; but this beatitude has been proven to be true, over and over again, in the case of persons who weep with a poverty-stricken spirit. "Blessed are they that mourn: for they shall be comforted." They shall be comforted here, and in the hereafter, "God shall wipe all tears from their eyes and there shall be no more crying."

> *"Did Christ o'er sinners weep,*
> *And shall our cheeks by dry?*
> *Let floods of penitential grief*
> *Burst forth from every eye.*
>
> *"The Son of God in tears,*
> *The wondering angels see;*
> *Be thou astonished, O, my soul,*
> *He shed those tears for thee.*
>
> *"He wept that we might weep,*
> *Each sin demands a tear;*
> *In heaven alone no sin is found,*
> *And there's no weeping there."*

Where Heaven Touches Earth.
Blessed are the meek: for they shall inherit the earth.
(Matt. 5:5)

Chapter IV

The Beatific Verity On Meekness.

If I should come to this intelligent congregation this morning and say that black is white, right is wrong, east is west, good is bad, up is down, heat is cold, height is depth, you would be unanimous in the opinion that I am a very foolish person. Why would you be of such an opinion? Because my expressions contradict all your ideas with reference to what I am talking about. Now such a statement from me would receive just as hearty acceptance and agreement from you as the statement made in this text received from the audience who heard it. It contradicted all their conceptions as to strength and inheritance. They thought the meek would never be the ones who received this inheritance. Nor can we say that this conception of things is confined to the First Century. Even in the Twentieth Century there are those who share this paganistic, materialistic view. This wrong view as to inheritance, as then held by most of the people, and by some even today, grows out of a misconception of four things: real meekness, true inheritance, human nature and the future. These things seen in their true light will bring the whole race to the viewpoint of our Savior, when he said, "Blessed are the meek: for they shall inherit the earth."

* * * * * * * * * * * *

Just what our Savior meant here in the word, meek, is a matter of dispute. It seems to me we have tried to narrow the term to suit some theory or plan of outline. Some, following Lange, try to force a meaning into the whole arrangement of the beatitudes, which will take the first as fundamental and the last as a conclusion, which is true; but then they will go further and try to have three of the remaining beatitudes refer to inner virtues and three to outer characteristics. This is not true without forcing the meaning and giving a mechanical interpretation. Our Savior could not have had this in mind. To do this, the term "meekness" must have only an outward interpretation. It means more than that, or it means but little to us. Nor can we say it has only an inner meaning. Most inner virtues have an outward significance, and this is true of meekness. But to say it means gentleness and no more, is to say what Jesus did not say. There are many forms of gentleness which cannot be meekness. One may be gentle from fear, or from economy, or from ignorance: this is not meekness at all.

The viewpoint of the world is that meekness is a negative virtue, and while it does not say so in just these words, it really thinks meekness is weakness. Needless to say, our Savior had no such idea in mind when he said that the meek should inherit the earth. There are four elements brought out in the use of the word we translate meek, and these four are one.

The first idea it carries is that of freedom from pretense, as opposed to the self-sufficient and the arrogant of the world. This idea is brought out in the first beatitude; of course this beatitude is a broader one than the first, and is not so fundamental. This freedom from pretense is necessary to the inheritance in any realm. As you enter the laboratory to try to inherit the wonderful knowledge about the shell, the flower, or the body of man or beast, this lesson is your first one. If you come with your own preconceived ideas, you shall inherit nothing. Science has no secrets to tell to any except the meek. The meek shall inherit the earth scientifically. You cannot be dogmatic in a scientific laboratory; you must in this realm do away with freedom of pretense. What is true in the realm of science is true of music, of art, of history, and everything else in the field of learning. You must be meek to learn things. If you think you know when you do not, then you shall never know at all. You must know that you do not know in order that you may know.

Another element entering into this term "meekness," which is very closely akin to the first, is the term "submissiveness." You remember Carlyle's remark when he heard some one say that Margaret Fuller accepted the universe, "Gad! She'd better." But it is one thing to accept it on compulsion, and another on choice. Prof. James, in his Varieties of Religious Experience, brings out this distinction very clearly. The world is full of people who are not submissive, who do not accept their lot without complaining. They are dissatisfied with God and with men, and with God's dealings with men. The meek man is one who recognizes God's thoughts to be above man's thoughts, and his ways to be higher than man's ways, and who accepts the universe. He can say with the Christ in the Garden, "Not my will, but thine be done."

Now these inner feelings and attitudes find an outward expression in two ways: the first of these is gentleness. The meek man is gentle. The gentle, whose gentleness grows out of freedom from pretense and submissiveness to God's will, and not from a lower motive, shall inherit the earth. This gentleness is the highest expression of strength. A weak person cannot possess such gentleness; it requires strength to exercise self-control and poise. A little soul may fret and shout from the house tops, but a great soul does not go off in a fit of anger and seek the destruction of all who do not come up to his standards of right. The nations of the world need just such meek men, of strength and poise, for leader and rulers. If such strength had been in the characters of the crowned heads of Europe, she today would not be the scene of such a bloody struggle. The Bible and civilization are a protest against animalism and brute force. You may judge a man's place in civilization by his meekness. Man's first ambition was to be a great animal. The Spartans were great Spartans if they could kill and steal successfully. Sampson was the hero of an age when might made right; but we do not consider Jess Willard and Jack Johnson our typical American heroes; we consider them great animals, somewhat superior to the horse or elephant. But we place in our first list those who have great brains and great hearts. The school boy progresses from the period when he loves to show his muscle, to where he loves to improve his mind. "He that is slow to anger is better than the mighty, and he that ruleth his spirit than he that taketh a city."

The second outward manifestation to this admirable inward attitude is patience. This is much akin to gentleness. To wait on the Lord and not to rush in where angels fear to tread—this is meekness in our Christ's mind.

Such meekness, our Christ showed forth in his life. He was never over-pretentious; he was always submissive to God's will and way. According to his own words, he came to do God's will. As a result of this inner tranquility, he was as gentle as the summer breezes and as patient as the human imagination can picture one as being. He was always biding his time; and an oft-repeated saying of his is, "My time is not yet come."

****

Now what was the idea of Jesus as touching inheritance? Did he mean that his followers should own the whole land and have title deeds to all countries? I hardly think he meant this. Our Savior began this beatitude by saying, "Blessed." If one is to own the earth, this ownership is to carry happiness. Now we know by observation that to own earthly possessions does not bring happiness. It does not necessarily keep one from being happy, but it does not of itself bring this blessedness to which our Christ is referring. And, besides, such ownership is not obtained in this way.

I think it would be more in accordance with his meaning to say that he meant by 'inherit the earth,' to control the earth. Who inherited the earth from Greece in the days of Plato? Was it some warrior, or some great landowner? Without consulting your books name me some of these great warriors and some of these slave-holders and land-owners. You cannot do it; but when we look into our schools and see Plato's thoughts studied and expressed by all the students, we know who inherited the earth from that period: it was a man whose ideas and ideals were handed down to posterity.

Who inherited the earth from Egypt in the days of Moses? Was it the ruling Pharaoh who owned the whole country, who even owned the bodies of millions of slaves? How many think of his ownership today? Was it really ownership? To be ownership it must be permanent. The man in this time who did not own one foot of earth, was the man who inherited the earth—Moses.

When the Romans conquered the Greeks, who really conquered, the ones who dictated the terms of peace? No, not in the fullest sense; for Greek ideas were soon taught in Rome, and Greek culture was brought over to the Imperial City. Rome had become Hellenized, and while Greece was defeated in battle, she inherited the earth of the conquerors.

In the days of early conflict between Roman Caesars and Christian martyrs, who conquered? The bodies of the Christians seemed weak indeed as compared with the mighty armies of the Caesars. The result was that Christianity seemed to be destroyed. But was it? The Roman men of arrogance and bloodshed no doubt thought the Christian principles and ideas the weakest of all things in the whole empire; but when the city fell, what was the one thing that did not fall? It was the Christian religion. The armies were conquered, the Senate was dissolved, the buildings were destroyed, but this Christian religion remained and stood. Its strength lay in its meekness, and it inherited the earth in that day.

****

Personally I have no doubt as to the outcome of the Christian religion, if we, as followers of Christ, stay by his principles and live his ideals. We cannot improve on his methods. The knowledge of the Lord shall cover the earth, as the water cover the sea, provided we shall be meek, for there is no truer statement anywhere that, "Blessed are the meek: for they shall inherit the earth."

The Discipline Of Discontent
Blessed are they which do hunger and thirst after righteousness: for they shall be filled (Matt. 5:6)

Chapter V

The Beatific Verity On Spiritual Dissatisfaction.

The Bible is a book of many figures, and the understanding of these figures is necessary to the understanding of the Bible. Of all the expressions or thought in the Bible where words used in the physical sense are applied to the spiritual, none is stronger than the 6th verse of the 5th chapter of Matthew, which reads, "Blessed are they which do hunger and thirst after righteousness: for they shall be filled." The strongest desires of our physical nature are those of hunger and thirst. Not only are they the strongest desires, but they are the most familiar; all know their force and significance. The small child who cannot yet speak the words "hunger" and "thirst" knows the desire for water and food. The most aged, who have reached the place "when they be afraid of that which is high, and fears shall be in the way, and the almond tree shall flourish, and the grasshopper shall be a burden, and desire shall fail"-even they know full well the force of hunger and thirst. These desires remain as long as life shall last. Some longings are confined to savages and others are experienced by the cultured only: but these desires are as well known and as forcibly felt in the jungle as in the king's mansion. Jesus especially knew the meaning of the statement at this time, as he had, according to Matthew's arrangement, just finished a forty-day fast in the wilderness of temptation.

Now there are three hungers and three thirsts in the world. There is first the physical hunger and thirst; all recognize this, and try to satisfy the calls of the physical man. Then there is the mental hunger and thirst. Most people recognize this as a real demand on the part of mental humanity, and endeavor to satisfy this call of our being. The last and highest hunger and thirst is the spiritual, which some recognize as a part of our being, and endeavor to satisfy their soul. Now I maintain that the least recognized is the most important, and the most recognized is the least important. The first two longings are for the sake of the last one; they occupy the same place with reference to the last one that the scaffold occupies to the house. Why do we eat, simply to have an opportunity of eating? Why do we study, simply to know? I tell you this is not the reason. We may eat to live, but we do not live to eat; only animals do this. Our acquiring knowledge is not simply for the sake of the knowledge, but to put that knowledge to some use and help humanity with it. The first two hungers are for the sake of the last one.

The first beatitude is fundamental with respect to this one, as it is with respect to all the others. We have poverty of spirit first, then hunger and thirst afterward; poverty, of course, in all realms, precedes hunger and thirst.

What do we mean by righteousness? Some say right doing, but this is not true. Righteousness is not concerned with results, but with motives, while right doing is concerned only with results and not with motives at all. If we strip this term "righteousness" of all theories men have piled around it, we can see its meaning. Nothing here is said about that mysterious element we call "imputed righteousness." This was not known for many hundred years after Christ. Righteousness means rightness, or the occupying of right relations to God, self, the world and all things else, even the devil and sin. All nobleness and genuine Christ-likeness flow from a relation of a human being right with God.

We notice in this verse a great demand; this demand is for God and for the soul to occupy the right relations to him. This demand grows right up in the soul of every person who is a responsible human being, whether he lives in the islands of the South Sea or the cold snows of Alaska. This is as real and as natural as a desire for a drink or food. Religion has always occupied, and always will occupy, the chief place in the thinking of all peoples. This is true because the soul's call for God is not a part of custom, but of nature. The advance of knowledge has changed some forms of worship, as it changes the kinds of food we eat, but it has not dulled this inner compulsion of the soul, any more than it has done away with the physical appetites of the race. Eugene Field, in his little poem, "The Wanderer," expressed a fundamental truth when he referred to a sea shell away on the top of the mountain,

"Strange, was it not? Far from its native deep
One song it sang-
Sang of the awful mysteries of the tide,
Sang of the misty sea, profound and wide,
Ever with echoes of the ocean rang.

"And as the shell upon the mountain height
Sings of the sea,
So do I ever, leagues and leagues away-
So do I ever wandering where I may-
Sing, O my home! Sing, O my home! Of thee."

The human soul pants for God as the hart pants for the waterbrook.

Not only do we see a demand, but the pain and urgency of it determine, in a large measure, our appreciation of its satisfaction. The soul that has loved much is the one, according to Christ, that has been forgiven much. If we are forgiven much, we must feel our need of forgiveness in a like proportion.

This demand is a continuous demand. Like the call for food and water, the desire for spiritual sustenance is perpetual. God had to send manna daily to satisfy his early children. Now Christ is the bread which came down from heaven, of which a man may eat and not die. Christ told us to pray for daily bread.

* * * * * * * *   * * * * * * * *

We also see a lack on our part with respect to satisfying this demand. Had man the ability to automatically satisfy his thirst and hunger, without that which is without him, there would be no hunger and thirst. So man cannot alone, or with other human beings, satisfy the call of his soul; the soul demands something outside of itself. That something is the righteousness of God.

* * * * * * * * * * * *

There is also a great sequel with respect to our passage. If a person has a strong desire to possess righteousness, he has an equally strong desire to get rid of sin and wrong. If you long for summer to be here with its birds and flowers, you long just as strongly for winter to leave with its snows and ice. If you look anxiously for the rising of the sun with his bright rays and warmth, you are just as anxiously looking for the night to depart with its darkness and chill. This is what Prof. James calls a forced option; you cannot long for the one without longing for the other. Our text tells us the person is blessed who has this longing. Why? Because he has taken the first step toward being satisfied. The hungry person is the one who eats. This principle holds good physically, mentally, and spiritually. The person who is in right relations with God and the world, is the person who is really happy. If he does not have the hunger of that which follows it-the satisfaction- he cannot be happy, but, on the other hand, is quite disappointed in what life gives to him. For a rose bush to be a success, it must bear roses after its nature. For a bird to be a success and happy, it must sing the songs of its tribe. For one bird to try to live the life of another, is to make that bird a failure. So God has put this innate longing in the human soul, and it must be met, or humanity is both unhappy and unsuccessful.

Any other satisfaction except that which the Maker of the soul has planned, will not satisfy. A man who has made a piece of machinery knows how to provide the missing piece. There is a story told of an old castle in Europe, in which there was a strange musical instrument, but no one could get any music from it. All who passed by this castle were called in to try this strange instrument. At last a stranger passed by, who knew the secret locks and the otherwise unknown laws with reference to it, and it was then made to give forth beautiful music; he was the maker of the instrument. This is but a legend, and, of course, untrue, but it illustrates the thought. Only the Maker knows what will satisfy, and he has told that to us. The experience of the race verifies the Maker's statement about it. Hungry travelers in Africa, on one occasion, found a bag of pearls. When they saw the bag, they in haste opened it, expecting to find food, but to their disappointment it was only pearls; these pearls, though a fortune, could not satisfy their hungry bodies. Nothing can fill the longing of the human heart but Jesus and what he gives.

* * * * * * * * * * * *

You can tell the strength of any desire by what one is willing to give up to satisfy it. If you are in poor health, and your physician tells you what you need to do to get your strength restored, the world can judge how much you want your health, by whether or not you do as you are bidden, to be restored. We judge how much our forefathers wanted liberty by what they were willing to undergo to procure it. You can judge religious desires and longings by a like standard. We can judge how much you want righteousness by how willing you are to pay the price of receiving it. The strength of your hungering and thirsting after God is determined by what you are willing to do to have this hunger satisfied, and this thirst quenched.

A Merciful Christ In An Unmerciful Age
Blessed are the merciful: for they shall obtain mercy
(Matt. 5:6)

Chapter VI

The Beatific Verity On The Merciful.

As a man walked down a road in Africa some years ago, a boy, we are told, threw a rock at him. The man picked up the rock, and, on examination, found it to contain precious diamonds.

In ages of the world's progress we often see the purest and most unselfish ideas expressed when we least expect them. Of all the ages in history when we would not have expected the beatitude on the merciful to be expressed, is the First Century. This being true makes us ask an old question: "Does the age shape ideas, or do ideas shape the age?" This question has been answered both ways. Some tell us that the age shapes ideas; that people generally believe as their contemporaries believe. When men as a whole want democracy, each man wants it. When the people as a whole want monarchy, each man wants it. Most of us fall in with public sentiment and drift with the tide. When the munition factories, with a few politicians, desire preparedness, the whole population rises up as one man and patriotically demands such. Preachers even march in preparedness parades. When the people as a whole accept anything as their life principle, it is because it is in the air as popular. But on the other hand, there are those in the world who do not accept the ideas and standards of an age, but who think for themselves and express their thoughts freely. Instead of accepting the ideas of the age in which they live, they express their own ideas, which will help to make the standards of coming ages. Now the ideas of Jesus were not according to First Century standards, but they militated against such standards.

What was the standard of the First Century civilization of mercy? It is well to look into this civilization and see what elements entered into it, and then see if each of these elements was conducive to mercy. There were three elements entering into this life as it was lived in this part of the Roman world in the First Century. The cultural life was the gift of the Greeks. They had given their poets and their philosophers to the world, and the thoughts of their fertile brains, as well as the beautiful language from their eloquent lips, became a legacy of the First Century. Did this life of culture and art, as given by ancient Greece, make people any more merciful? We say, No. It was bigoted and self-sufficient. If anyone ventured to disagree with the person in power, off would go his head or he would be sent into exile. It was Greek culture carried to its conclusion that compelled Socrates to drink the hemlock. Greek philosophers said repeatedly that to hold slaves was a necessity, that time might be had for culture and thought.

Another element entering into the civilization as it was lived in Palestine in the days of Jesus, was Roman law. Was it helpful to the merciful? No; it, too, was most unmerciful in all realms. A Roman father had the right to kill a son if he pleased to do it, and was not noticed by the law for so doing. Cicero concedes this, and then expresses his opinion as favoring the same right with respect to an adopted son. Valerius Maximus tells of fathers who slew sons and gives the names of the sons. Plutrach refers to

Casius Brutus who put to death a son for disobedience. The father had the same right with respect to the life of his daughter, and also his wife. A wife often ran a long pin into the arm of a servant because of disobedience. There are pages reeking with blood, telling us of Roman cruelty in the home life. Brace, in his Gesta Christa, devotes many pages to this.

Another element enters into the age in which Jesus lived, was the Jewish religion. Of all things militating to shape ideals, we should have thought that the religion of the Jew would have been a merciful religion. David, although a man of blood, and a self-confessed murderer, uses the term "mercy" over a fourth of a hundred times, in his songs. In the Old Testament, God is referred to hundreds of times as being full of mercy, and this same loving trait is commended to his children. But the First Century evidently had a very short memory for these Old Testament passages which spoke of mercy, and a keen memory for the bloody passages of the Old Bible. It was the most orthodox Jew who scorned most the sinner and outcast, and who shamefully treated the Samaritan. It was the leaders in orthodoxy in Jerusalem who agitated the crucifixion of Jesus, and who took the lead in persecution of the disciples. Christ recognized this lack of mercy in Jewish religious thought, in his parable of the Good Samaritan. The man who gave the least attention to the wounded, was the man highest up in Jewry. The man who gave a little more attention, but not enough, was the man next in the scale. The third man, who was really merciful, was one who did not pretend to be religious at all, according to the Jewish standards. The more Jewish a person was, according to this standard of Christ, the less merciful he was. The farther away from Jewish thought and life a person was, the more merciful he was to his fellow men. The parable shows the First Century Jew unmerciful in the thoughts, attitudes, religious feelings, and deeds, toward his fellows. I do not care to be misunderstood here; the Twentieth Century Jew is not the First Century Jew by a great deal; the present Jew is, as a rule, kind and generous. Many make good citizens in all free governments, and are loyal subjects in all monarchies. But this is not due to what they receive from their religion; it is due to Christian progress that has touched the Jew, as well as others. Shakespeare's opinion of the Jew in European life was not that he was a man of mercy.

Portia: *"Then must the Jew have mercy?"*
Shylock: *"On what compulsion must I? Tell me that."*
Portia: *"The quality of mercy is not strained.*
It droppeth as the gentle rain from heaven
Upon the place beneath; it is twice blest;
It blesseth him that gives and him that takes,
'Tis mightiest in the mightiest; it becomes
the throned monarch better than his crown.
His scepter shows the force of temporal power.
The attribute to awe and majesty,
Wherein doth sit the fear and dread of kings.
But mercy is above his sceptered sway,
It is enthroned in the hearts of kings,
It is the attribute to God himself;
And earthly power doth then how likest God's
When mercy seasons justice."

This is a fair sample of the contrast between the Christian ideal and the Jewish. So we see that the First Century, with its Greek culture, Roman law, and Jewish religion, did not shape this verse.

****

Our Savior began his work by assaulting cruelty. In his day, "man's inhumanity to man made countless millions mourn." But he went against such inhumanity every time he had an opportunity. The sick, the dying, and the children were special objects of his care. The outcasts were treated with mercy, though such treatment brought down on the head of Jesus the most unmerciful criticism. In Ben Hur, General Wallace does not have the Savior speak where the Bible keeps him silent. Those long years between the boy in the temple at the age of twelve and the public appearance, were unbroken by any recorded word from the lips of Jesus. It was during this period the Ben Hur was dragged through the village of Nazareth on the way to the galleys for life. Some have said that when Christ met Gen Hur at the well, if Mr. Wallace had put into his mouth a single word he would have ruined the book. He does not put into his mouth a word, but he does put into his thought a noble deed. He has him give a drink of water to the crushed young man lying there in the dust. He does have him do that which forms quite a contrast to the cruelty of the Roman.

****

Jesus inspired his disciples to exercise a similar mercy toward all men. The early Christians caught this view of the thing. They were known as people who had mercy in their lives. The most unmerciful thing in the world then was the roman arena. The ruins of the Coliseum still stand as a silent monument to Roman cruelty and Christiona mercy. We are taught that eighty thousand people could get into this noted place at one time. A special seat was reserved for the emperor with his cruel friends. Here both man and beast suffered, bled, and died. Ten thousand gladiators were slain during the inaugural fete of one Caesar. The Christians would never go about the place except on compulsion. They hated the bloodshed and cruelty; their Master had said, "Blessed are the merciful." Through Christian teaching spreading over the world, the cruelty was temporarily stopped, but only stopped to begin again. One day, a men were falling on the white sand, reeking with gore, a man threw himself over the parapet and rushed between the slayers and halted them with his rebuke; many spears entered his body at once. On examination, it was found to be Telemachus, a good Christian man. From that time on, bloodshed in the arena was numbered with the things that Christian civilization has thrown away. The preaching of the gospel of Jesus has struck fetters from the wrists of millions of slaves, made home life happy, enacted laws of tolerance and mercy, opposed the oppression of the poor, and is busy now in outlawing the saloon and giving to women their rights to citizenship. People who have taken Christ's words seriously are they who are merciful in the world. Europe is not deluged in blood today because she is Christian in ideals, but because she is not Christian in ideals. To enter a battle in the Twentieth Century by prayer is as absurd as opening up a saloon at your mother's grave or selling a white slave at a church bazaar. Tolstoy read these words of Jesus and seriously believed them worth following. He followed them by selling his possessions and giving his money to the poor; he took a peasant's hut in which to live and work; he toiled in the field with the people who were poor but honest. For thirty years, it is said that he went by the name of the "Organized Conscience of Russia." He was excommunicated from the Russian Church and rebuked by the Czar; but instead of receiving the excommunication, as was expected, he laughed and said the church had excommunicated itself; and instead of receiving the rebuke of the Czar, as was expected, he sent a sharper one to him than was received by Tolstoi; the Czar was afraid to answer. He denounced the cruelty of Siberia and the intolerance of the Russian people. Why did he take this view? He took Jesus at his word and believed the Sermon on the Mount was a true document and tried to live it every day. Christianity is responsible for the white-robed nurses, the skilled physicians, the sanitary hospitals, and all the agencies of mercy in the world. Real Christians are merciful in their thoughts and judgments, in their speech and deeds.

* * * * * * * * * * *

Sometimes here mercy is met with cruelty, and kind words with abuse, but is will not always be so. Hereafter, when the God of all mercy shall come in the glory of the morning, the merciful shall receive mercy. But we who hold to Christian optimism do not think we shall have to wait till that blessed day to see a reign of mercy. We think we have made almost enough progress now to recognize that mercy begets mercy, and loving words call forth loving words. If a person gives the best he has to the world now, we believe the best will come back again. We fully expect a reign of mercy on earth.

>   For I dipt into the future,
>   Far as human eye could see,
>   Saw the Vision of the world, and
>   All the wonder that would be.
>
>   Till the war drum throbbed no longer,
>   And the battle flags were furled
>   In the Parliament of man,
>   The Federation of the world.

The Vision Of The Pure
Blessed are the pure of heart: for they shall see God
(Matt. 5:6)

Chapter VII

The Beatific Verity On The Pure In Heart.

A scene is now before my mind that I have often wished I could remove, because every time I think of the occasion, my heart is filled with sadness. I was going through a prison and saw a life prisoner telling his little girl goodbye. As the darling child threw her pretty, white arms around his neck, tears poured form her baby eyes. In the background was the darkness of the prison, dimly dotted with cells. In each cell stood a man with sad face, and despondent visage. This innocent child, with full warm tears of love and sadness running down her cheeks, with such a background, formed a picture of contrast noticeable, indeed.

Dr. Jowett tells of plucking a bunch of violets from a clump of thistles. We sometimes see a sunbeam dancing in a slimy cave. Such a contrast as the ones just mentioned is brought forth in this text: "Blessed are the pure in heart: for they shall see God." It was the most sinful and depraved age that civilization has ever seen. It was the dirtiest of ages, and the most impure of thought and life. Home life was debased, and "in the corrupted currents of this political world, offenses' guilded hand had shoved by justice" Who would expect such a sentence in such an age? This text, like Portia's little candle, throws its beams affar, like a good deed in a naughty world.

Now life, as has been said many times before, is made up of fundamentals and incidentals. This text deals exclusively with fundamentals. Jesus show by this passage his relation to these fundamentals of life as brought forth in the text.

The fundamental of human happiness is spoken of in this text, and Christ shows how to achieve this much-sought-after condition of life. " Blessed are the pure in heart." As we have observed, "blessed" means to be happy in the highest sense. This happiness, which is the object of the quest of the human race, according to Jesus, is inward rather than outward. A man's happiness is hinged on his inner life and motives; in order for one to be blessed, he must be pure in heart.

The New Testament use of the word we translate "heart" is not as narrow as we make it. We usually speak of the heart as the seat of the emotional nature. The feelings arise from this source, but not man's intellectual conceptions and volitional purposes. But Jesus did not narrow the meaning thus; his use of the word included all of man's mental and moral nature. When he spoke of a man's heart being pure, he meant that a man's thoughts must be pure, his motives must be pure, and, of course, his emotions would, as a result, be pure. The Jews, to whom he was speaking, had emphasized ceremonial purity, but Christ sees a more important purity for seeing God-this heart purity.

With this understanding of the terms, we can plainly see that it is the heart that sees God and sees anything else. It is the heart that hears, also. The ears help and the eyes help, but while they help they are dependent on the heart to do the real work of hearing and seeing. You may have your eyes focused on an object and never see it, and your ears may be reporting to your brain a thousand sounds of which you do not take notice.

The heart does the seeing, but not unless it is a pure heart with reference to what is seen. Drugs are pure if they are what they are supposed to be, with no other substances contained. So with water; it is pure when it is just water; so with air or anything else. To have a pure view, you must have a single view, a view free from foreign substance. "If thine eye be single, thy whole body shall be full of light." If thine eye be double then thou hast an impurity of vision which will give thee false impressions. The double-minded man of James was a man whom we expect to find unstable in all his ways. In our expectations we were right; what he lacked was a purity, which was necessary to the giving of accuracy. Whether or not you see anything depends on your singleness, or purity, or your freedom from foreign substance with reference to it. A lady laughed the other night as Frederick Ward reached his climax in presenting Richard the Third. Poor soul. She saw all she could see with respect to such things. Perhaps she could have told the difference between a cabbage and an onion. I heard a lady express a wish to be at the picture show, the other evening, as Theobaldi played. Those who sat about her also wished she had gone to some other place than where she was then. You do not see a picture, a piece of statuary, or a heroic deed or a poem, or anything, without purity of your perceiving power with respect to that certain thing.

The wish to see God is as old as the race. This wish expressed itself in the olden times by the making of idols, and by even the crudest forms of worship. This wish, as it expressed itself, called forth the commandment,"Thou shalt not make unto thee any graven image." It was the making of such images that portrayed to the world the thoughts of the people. But to see God is not a physical possibility. No dullard with respect to spiritual things can see God. Wordsworth's boy, of whom he said:

"A primrose on a river's brim,,
  A yellow primrose was to him,
    And it was nothing more."

could not see in the beauty of the flower the thoughts that lie too deep for words. So no man can hope to see God in his holiness as long as he has double vision of earth. The astronomers have searched in vain for the Bethlehem Star. It is a star of the soul and not one of the telescope; they will never find it; there were thousands who were sleeping under it who never saw it, while a few who were hundreds of miles away caught glimpses of it radiance.

    God can be partly seen here, if we are pure in heart. All nature shows God to us. "Every bush is aflame with God, but only he who sees, takes off his shoes." This earth is patterned after the kingdom of heaven very closely. Now this is an axion which we may follow: "If two times four equal eight, then four times two equal eight." We all see it. Then see something just as plain in Christ's teachings, "The kingdom of heaven is like a mustard seed, a sower in the field, a drag net, and many other things." That being true, if the kingdom of heaven is like these things, they in turn are like the kingdom of heaven. People of the crudest type have seen this truth, but because they went too far we have swung over to an equally absurd view of nature.

"Back of the loaf is the snowy flour,
  Back of the flour, the mill;
  Back of the mill the wheat and shower,
  And the sun and the Father's Will."

Again he is a man blind to spiritual truths who does not see God in the unfolding of human history. One increasing purpose runs through the lives of men and nations. The real historian of today does not look at events as separated from everything else. He looks out movements. He tries to trace the mind of God through the lives of men in the world. Our God is a God of history; he made the world, but he never has absented himself from it. He is in the world now as really and powerfully as when Abraham was called from the Ur of the Chaldees, or when Joseph was placed in an Egyptian prison. He has just as much to do with the small things of our lives as he had to do with the interpretation Joseph made of the dreams of the Pharaoh. In those days the pure in heart were so few that they were noticed more than now, when they are so many that we do not think about it. It is said that in St. Paul's in London are these words, "If you desire to see the monument of Sir Christopher Wren, look around you." So if you desire to see God, read history with a mind free from the foreign substances of prejudices. He is there for any man to see who has purity enough to behold him.

The pure man sees God in the lives of good people. Every Christian is a revelation of the God who made and converted him. If the dying Bunsen saw the Eternal in his wife's eyes as he said he did, then all persons with pure hearts can see God in the people who serve him and carry out his message. God is in every kind word, every gentle deed, and even every cup of cold water given in his name. If you do not see him it is not his fault, but yours.

To the person of proper vision, God was in Christ reconciling the world to himself. "He that hath see me hath seen the Father"; these are the words of our Christ. What did he mean? Did Judas see the Father, did Pilate, or did Herod? I do not think so. They did not see Jesus, was the reason. The persons who thought he was just a Galilean peasant did not see him; the ones who saw only the loaves and fishes did not see him. They saw the carpenter from Nazareth, but they did not see Jesus the Christ, the Son of the Living God. They did not see him because they did not have a purity of mental and spiritual vision, which was necessary to seeing him then, as well as now. When Peter said, "Thou art the Christ, the Son of the living God," Jesus said, "Flesh and blood hath not revealed this unto thee." This is true even now, as Dean Stanley said in the last sermon he ever preached, which was from this, our text. He said: "The single eye and the pure conscience are an indispensable condition of having the doors of our minds open and the channel of communication kept free between us and the supreme and eternal fountain of all purity and of all goodness."

     But Jesus said that no man had seen God at any time. What did he mean by this statement? He meant that our present glimpses of God are partial and most imperfect. If we could be perfectly pure in heart we should see God in the beauty of his holiness. As Chas. Kingsley lay dying, he said: "How beautiful is God." Perhaps this is but the earnest of his vision. "It doth not yet appear what we shall be, but we know that when he shall appear, we shall be like him, for we shall see him as he is." May we turn this statement around a little?---when we get to be like him we shall see him as he is. We see him here in proportion to our purity of heart, be when we are perfectly like him, then we shall see him as he is.

> *"Some day the silver cord will break,*
> *And I no more as now shall sing:*
> *But, O, the joy when I awake*
> *Within the palace of the King."*

Swords Into Plowshares
Blessed are the peacemakers: for they shall be called the children of God (Matt. 5:9)

Chapter VIII

The Beatific Verity On The Peacemakers.

Jesus was reared in a powder mill. Members of his race who were reared in this powder mill were all the time striking matches and doing all in their power to cause an explosion. Some who tried this succeeded to a degree, but did not reach the point of success that entirely blew up existing conditions. Judas Maccabeus struck the match with marked success, but the result of the explosion was only for a comparatively brief time.

The friends and admirers of Jesus, from the very first, thought he had come to strike another match in this powder mill. They were ready to hail him as Messiah, if he could successfully consummate a revolution. "Wilt thou at this time restore the kingdom of Israel?" was an oft repeated question. John the Baptist fully expected Christ to strike the match, and when he in prison learned that this match had not been struck, he was very much disappointed. Because of his disappointment he sent a number of his disciples to Jesus to learn if he were the Messiah they had hoped he was. In his preaching about Christ he had said: "His fan is in his hand." Was he putting the ax to the root of the tree as the forerunner had said he would put the ax to the root of the tree? Perhaps his own disciples said to him: "Your Messiah is doing nothing you said he would do, and many thing you said nothing about." The mother of Zebedee's children expected he would strike the match some day, and thought she would prepare for the occasion by having her sons occupy the first place in the new kingdom when that time came. She thought he was the logical person to do this thing. Simon the Zealot, no doubt, joined himself to the party of Christ because of his revolutionary hopes. He was a member of a party pledged to throw off the yoke. Christ reached his summit of popularity when the expectations of such an uprising were highest in the minds of the people. The nominal, superficial followers of Christ scattered from him as sheep from a shepherd, when they saw he would not strike the match. The going away was so general that Christ asked if the disciples also would go away.

If we fully understand this historical situation, it will throw floods of light on Judas and his character. He was a worldly-minded man, who had full hopes that Jesus would strike the match and cause this prayed-for and long-expected revolution. When it dawned on him that this was not what Jesus was going to do, disappointment and resentment held full sway in his sordid mind. How could a soul so mercenary and materialistic as was his, appreciate and love a spiritual Messiah?

Now a strange thing is this, that if Jesus struck the match, as most of his admirers expected he would do, it would have been yielding to the Satanic temptations of the wilderness. The first thing he had to decide completely, on entering his public work, was whether or not he would strike this match. Every temptation in a way asked him to do this, and based the request on the prerogatives of Sonship to God. When he came from the wilderness it was settled definitely. His mind was not to be changed, no matter how many of his disciples should persuade, or good women urge, or fast friends misunderstand and doubt, or relatives malign. It was settled once for all. Thank God, it was settled right. The substance of the settlement is in the text: "Blessed are the peacemakers: for they shall be called the children of God." When he uttered these words, it struck disappointment to the hearts of many who heard them, even among his friends and admirers. I doubt if he could have brought a more disappointing message than the one contained in the text.

The people of the First Century never heard of getting anything in this way. All the lands of the Roman Empire had been secured through armies and killing. Even the land that once flowed with milk and honey, while a chosen land for them, they thought, had been gotten through bloodshed and battle. How could the Christ expect to establish his reign by saying: "Blessed are the peacemakers?" This is the historical meaning of the text. Does it have any significance today?

****

I think we can see some very fundamental principles in this passage. Our God is a God of peace. He is peaceful in his creative work, and peaceful in his redemptive work. Peace is music; discord is lack of peace. A piece of machinery makes music when it runs according to the maker's plan; when it is broken it causes lack of peace. Peace means harmony in any realm. A man who removes the causes of discord is a peacemaker, and is engaged in the same work that God is in, for God made the world to run harmoniously. "The morning stars once sang together." every normal human soul loves peace and good will.

It seems to me that this is the fundamental difference between laughter and weeping. Laughter is harmonious and we all love to hear it; crying is discord and we do not love to hear ti. God has made all persons to love harmony and hate discord, except when their souls have been narrowed or depraved or degraded by false standards and infamous teachings. God is a peace-loving Creator, and he has sent his anathemas against the people who destroy this peace.

* * * * * * * *

Jesus was a great restorer of peace when he was here. He met the weeping and removed the cause of their grief. His sensitive soul was shocked even with the rough, noisy waves of the the sea, and he hushed them into a great calm. His soul ached because of the misunderstandings of his disciples, and he settled their disputes. When he got ready to go away he wondered who should keep them in comfort and peace. He said: "My peace I leave with you." Again he said: "As I have loved you, love ye one another." He made all possible provisions for his people to be peaceful, for in being peaceful they would be God-like. He knew that God hated bloodshed and murder and wrangling, through the ancient people had claimed his authority and sanction for such conduct.

Since peace is a God-like and normal result of right conditions, then lack of peace is due to something being wrong. I think it is due to wrong thinking largely. It is decidedly ungod-like to imagine any one people are the chosen of the Lord, to the exclusion of all others. When Israel thought this of themselves, they marched to battle singing psalms as though such singing pleased a God who made even the ponderous planets to be peaceful in their movements. This habit of false thinking causes discord between labor and capital. The one is taught to believe that he is absolutely right and the other is taught to believe that he is absolutely right. Both hold false ideas, and as long as such ideas are held, misunderstanding will be the result.

Not only do we see wrong thinking, but also wrong talking, as a cause of discord. When people harbor wrong and envious thoughts about others, they usually find some manner of giving expression to these thoughts. We are hearing more foolish talking right now than has been heard in a century, with respect to the intentions and aims of nations. People do not have the hatred in their hearts that some false thinkers and foolish talkers would have you believe.

****

The fruits of peace are seen in all realms and walks of life. The evil fruits of war are also seen. You have heard the statement that war always brings out the best. This is as false as most things said about the benefits of war. If there is anything on earth that brings out the hell in the human soul, it is this outgrown institution we call war, and name it bravery; indeed, we should call it murder and name it crime. What brings out the best in anybody or anything is peace, not war. War never made a hero; it sometimes manifests one to the world, but never creates one. Peace is the brooding place for great men and women. The heroic type is all about us at all times, if we have eyes with which to see. The heroism of peace does not receive due recognition, while the heroism of war receives over-recognition. Why call a man a hero who dies in war trying to kill somebody else, while the one who toils from morning till night and lives a life of self-sacrifice that he may provide for his own, goes down with no words of praise spoken about him, and often sleeps in an unmarked grave? But our Christ knew that most of the real heroes of life would not be recognized as such, so he told them of a recognition that would be theirs some time when truth got a hearing and God's will was done: they should be called the children of God. This is more than wearing a Victorian Cross, or an Iron Cross, or any other distinction which comes from being a successful murderer.

Happy home life, honest business life, spiritual church life, pure social life, sincere educational life, and patriotic political life all come from conditions of peace in these realms, and seldom from conditions of war.

I think we should admire the heroes of war in the days of the past, but not admire them that we may duplicate them. They are all right because they do not live now. The world has outgrown them as it has outgrown slavery and other antique institutions. Call them honest, just like slaveholders were honest. Observe memorial days and lay flowers on their graves; put these flowers there for two reasons: first, because they have lived in the world and have done the best they knew; and second, that they went home in good time, and that we now know better how to serve our country and time.

****

Now to be a peacemaker and have the benediction of God abiding on us is a great boon. How do we become such? We must begin with this where our Savior began in his beatitudes, with poverty of spirit. This is the fundamental beatitude. The war makers and the persons who are arrogant and prejudiced, while the peacemakers are poor in spirit and liberal-minded. The kind of folk who create discord in all walks are those who do not have this poverty of spirit.

You must also be a lover of peace to be a peacemaker. One whose soul delights in strife and discord is seldom a peacemaker. The artist who touches the canvas and blends shades and colors, is the one who has a deep love for beauty and art. The musician who brings out sweet harmony from an instrument has a soul that is hurt when discord is heard, and on that rejoices in sweet harmony.

Not only so, but one must be able to know what peace is, and to show a full recognition of all forms of discord. He must follow up this knowledge with impartiality. The person who will not pay such a price has not this great blessing resting on him.

To be called the sons of God is a reward sufficient to satisfy all pure-minded people. This is the closest relation that could exist between the creature and the Creator. God help us to so have the peace of God in our souls, that we may carry this peace into all walks and realms of life, and to be real peacemakers for our peace-loving Father.

Lashed To A Great Cause
Blessed are they which are persecuted for righteousness' sake: for theirs is the kingdom of heaven. Blessed are ye when men shall revile you, and persecute you, and shall say all manner of evil against you falsely, for my sake. Rejoice and be exceeding glad: for great is your reward in heaven: for so persecuted they the prophets which were before you (Matt. 5:10-12)

Chapter IX

The Beatific Verity On The Persecuted For Righteousness' Sake.

The last beatitude in the Sermon on the Mount brings as a reward the same thing the first one brought. The first one said: "Theirs is the kingdom of heaven," and so with the last one.

Oliver Goldsmith, in his "Deserted Village," in speaking of his desire to return home to spend his last days, gave us this language:

> *"And as an hare, whom hounds and horns pursue,*
> *Pants to the place from whence at first she flew,*
> *I still had hopes, my long vexations past,*
> *Here to return, and die at home at last."*

He voices, in these poetic words, an eternal principle of life. Life, as Emerson observes, goes in circles. God made the world on such lines, and he makes ideals and dreams on the same lines. Jesus, true always to life, starts with a statement and then comes back to it for his conclusion. His fundamental beatitude, on which beatitude all the rest are builded, tells us that the persons who possess poverty of spirit are in present possession of the kingdom of heaven. Then he gives us six other characteristics of the ideal Christian, and what shall be to his person as a result. After this he crowns the whole of his structure with the relation this Christian sustains to the world about him, and comes back to the original statement that this strange person, this individual whose conscience is an alarm bell in the world, still possesses the kingdom of heaven.

All of the beatitudes contradicted existing opinions of things, and formed in themselves paradoxes. This is the most paradoxical of all, and the hardest one to believe. Since it is so hard to accept, he repeats it with emphasis. In his repetition he applies it to his disciples by saying: "Blessed are ye." Not only does he repeat it, and apply it, but he also advances arguments to establish it completely in the minds of his followers, for they are to stand much in need of the fundamental teaching contained in this verse of scripture. In his second statement of this rejoicing in persecution, he uses a very strong word with respect to being happy in persecution. He literally says: "Leap for joy."

This peculiar statement is very hard of comprehension by Twentieth Century Americans. The thumbscrew and the block are now outlawed as means of persecution of any religious sect. The country in which we live has insured to all generations religious freedom. For us to know fully what he meant by this statement, we must put ourselves back in the First Century and, in imagination, be Christians under Roman rule. Of the twelve sitting nearest him, only one was to die in his bed. Many of the other Christians sitting on this mountain side are to be thrown to wild beasts and torn asunder in the most agonizing way. The bodies of people who were hearing these words are to be covered with tar and made into torches for the lighting of cities. They are not only by their spiritual life to be lights in the moral world, but in their dying bodies they are to literally light the world as they burn to death.

But we must not get the idea that this verse has no present-day application. Persecution is not altogether in the immutable days of your. Men do not hurt with dagger, but the tongue of criticism is sharper than the keenest dagger. Fires of false statements burn more, and are harder to endure, than the fires of the Roman world could possibly be. There is hardly a city or village of any size, in which you cannot with ease find good men and women who have been maligned and ill-treated because of their loyalty to principle and to Jesus. Christianity is a message which opposes the hell of depraved human nature. Two cannot walk together except they be agreed. They are not agreed by nature and never will be, no matter how much progress the world has made or will make. One of two things, or both, may happen to help the situation and remove persecution, otherwise it will always be. The world may become more Christian, which would, of course, lessen persecution. It is becoming more Christian in ideals and standards, and in some places more Christian in deeds and lives. This will help. Again Christian standards may become more worldly. This is no doubt true. Now, while the little leaven of Christ and his message is doing its work, getting the whole leavened, we are compelled to admit that the devil is dulling the keen edge of the Gospel sword and bringing some of his standards over into Christian activity.

* * * * * * * * * * ** * * * * * *

Our Savior in this verse desired to show the blessedness of being lashed to a great cause. This cause, he wanted to teach, was greater and bigger and worth more than any one individual attached to it. It was not simply the persecution that brought one into the beatific condition, but to be attached to him, and be persecuted for righteousness sake. The biggest man in the whole world is a very little creature unless he is indissolubly united with a great cause for which he is willing to be spent and to give his best in life and, if need be, in death. We remember the noble dead and honor the noble living, because of their connection with noble causes. We do not remember Luther because he was an eloquent German. There were men of his day and in his country as eloquent as he was. He is in our minds because he attached himself to an undying cause. The same is true of Washington, Wesley, Lincoln and Lee. Now this cause, known as righteousness, is as old as God, and the opposition to it is as old as Man. The first act of Christ's public ministry was to identify himself with the cause of righteousness as proclaimed by John the Baptist, and to complete or fulfill that cause, hitherto incomplete. He sealed his loyalty to this movement with his blood, and in his teaching tied his disciples to it in life and, if need be , in death. The man who is thus united with this cause, which is bound in the end to win, is a most blessed, and also a most happy man. Though he be a Daniel in a lion's den, his inward peace makes him really happy. Though he be a Paul or a Silas in a prison, with blood on his back and with cuts of the lash in his sides, he can sing songs of joy unto our Father.

* * * * * * * * * * *

This blessedness comes from the character you possess, which responds to the call of the Christ and to the cause of righteousness. We honor any man who has character enough to stand for principle. Whether we agree with a person or not, we can see his greatness and bravery, and men admire such. We can see this life, thus lived and surrendered, is following principle and truth, rather than the tides of time. Such a life is bigger than any environment. We see a beautiful illustration of this truth in the life of Paul, the great Apostle. As he journeyed to Jerusalem that last time, on the coast at Miletus and at other places, he was told of the persecution and imprisonment which awaited him on his arrival, but he would not be persuaded, for none of these things moved him. He had a message to take to Jerusalem, and though the carrying of this message meant death, it must be carried. His was a boat that could go up stream.

Purpose is also seen in such a person. This purpose shows forth a Christian to the world as nothing else may. They have one thing to do, no matter what their lot on earth may be, and this one thing is to stand for the great cause of Christ and righteousness. This truth makes Christians the conscience of the world. Of course when persecutions arise, it makes the true Christian more God-like in their lives. Thomas Fuller said, "When men build this building, it is because there is no room to build on the ground." So when we have persecutions in the earth, and cannot build out in the world, as a result we are building up toward God.

* * * * * * * * * * * *

Then there comes the blessedness of being on opposite sides from the persons who persecute. In Hebrews we read a statement, "of whom the world was not worthy." Then would you not rather be with the element that is worthy than with the unworthy element of the world? Some people are loved because of the enemies they have made; and whether we admit it or not, some are honored because of the enemies they have made These enemies speak more eloquently than the most indulgent friends could possibly speak of their worth and characters.

* * * * * * * * * * *

Not only do we have the blessedness of being on the opposite side from the persons who are wrong, but we have the blessedness of being on the same side with the persons who are right. Jesus wants this truth impressed on the minds of his followers. "For so persecuted they the prophets who were before you" So, by going through persecution, you are classed with weeping Jeremiah, fiery Amos, and great Isiah. We have the fellowship of these inspiring minds.

> "There is one
> Great society on earth,
> The noble living and the noble dead."

In being a member of this great society you are a person really and truly blest, no matter what your lot on earth may be.

Jesus makes the cause of righteousness and the cause of Christ identical. This is as it should be. There never was a righteous thought, a holy motive, a noble deed, or a worthy institution that Jesus would not encourage. " In every nation he that feareth God and worketh righteousness, is accepted with him" To love Jesus and to surrender to him is to do a righteous deed.

Character Tree-Planting

Blessed is the man that walketh not in the counsel of the ungodly, nor standeth in the way of sinners, nor sitteth in the seat of the scornful. But his delight is in the law of the Lord; and in his law doth he mediate day and night. And he shall be like a tree planted by the rivers of water, that bringeth forth his fruit in his season; his leaf also shall not wither; and whatsoever he doeth shall proper (Ps. 1:1-3).

Chapter X

The Beatific Verity On True Manhood.

True manhood in the changing ages is like a piece of pure gold in the fire; both remain unchanged. Character is the most durable thing in the world. We are taught by the words of Jesus that a woman who on one occasion chose character instead of many passing things, really chose that which would never be taken away from her. Men have erected cities and have expected these cities to perpetuate their memories. They have in this made mistakes, for the cities have crumbled long ago, and yet these men are still remembered. Solomon built in Jerusalem great structures, but they have long since ceased to be. Solomon is as well known now as he was twenty centuries ago. Caesar built inrome, and many times led captive kings through her streets, but ancient Rome is about gone, yet Caesar is as well known now as he was a thousand years ago. Human beings in their characters are abiding, and this cannot be said of anything else that is touched with earth.

This beatitude is the most familiar in the Old Testament, "Blessed is the man that walketh not in the counsel of the ungodly, nor standeth in the way of sinners, nor sitteth in the seat of the scornful. But his delight is in the law of the Lord and in his law doth he meditate day and night. And he shall be like a tree planted by the rivers of water, that bringeth forth his fruit in his season; his leaf also shall not wither, and whatsoever he doeth shall prosper" (Ps. 1:1-3).

Like most beatitudes it contradicts existing notions of things. It was not always considered that the righteous man was the one who experienced prosperity. But the righteous, those who possess genuine character, are always admired, even by persons who are not righteous. And after these good people leave us and go to the other country, then we love to think about them and to fill our parks with their likenesses, and our hearts with their memories; for "the memory of the just is blessed."

* * * * * ** * * * * * * * * * * *

True manhood is blessed in what it is not. According to the passage given as the basis of this chapter, we learn what a righteous man is by learning what he is not. This negative definition is given in three parts and these three characteristics are arranged in a most logical manner. The first shows the righteous man in the realm of ideas, "walketh not in the counsel of the ungodly." He does not care to take their advice. Taking bad advice is, of course, the first downward step. You can tell what a man's character is by what advice he is willing to accept as forming a standard of life. Taking bad advice may not be much, for you are simply "walking" in their counsel, and walking is not permanent. Ideas may never amount to anything real and tangible. Many ideas have never gotten out of the brain of the man who possessed them. And yet all deeds come from ideas; if the ideas be bad, then the deeds are bad. If the ideas are pure, then the deeds are noble. The first step in a downward course is to walk in the counsel of the ungodly and to be advised by them.

The second step in the life of a person who is righteous, is in the realm of attitude, "standeth not in the way of sinners." this shows an advance step over the first one.

This unrighteous man is not walking, but has assumed an attitude, that of standing, more or less permanent. Ideas must be expressed in attitudes, or they will leave the mind entirely. Did the man who received the wrong counsel go no further it would not be so bad. When he has gotten to the place of attitude, he has gone pretty far. Life is indeed a matter of attitudes. The way you see a man inclined is the way he is apt to go; that shows his character.

The third step in the realm of the good person, is in the realm of deeds. An attitude must go still further to be all. It must go to the realm of acts. We see the unrighteous man reach a climax in that he is scornful and is permanent in his scorn. He sits in the seat of the scornful. Our righteous friend does not begin, continue, or finish the course of the ungodly. Turn these negative definitions around and you will see true manhood in its positive characteristics. He takes the advice of the godly, walks in the way of good company, and sits with "Christian optimists.

* * * * * * * * * * * * * ** * * *

True manhood is blessed in its delights, for our pleasures show our characters more than we think. "His delights are in the law of God." The good man is generally the happy man. He has more reasons for being happy than the man who lives an ungodly life. You may think of some Christians of peculiar temperament who are unhappy, but were they not Christians, they would be much more unhappy than they are at present. There is not one thing in religion to take happiness away form one. There are many things to bring happiness into one's life.

These delights show his love of goodness. To do good from the view point only of duty, is all right if you have no higher motive; but if you really love to do it, and find real pleasure in doing it, it will speak more for your character, and will make the work more successful. Most of the great things in life have been struck off at moments when people were intent on their work, and were really enjoying it.

Now our character mentioned here, was one who delighted in law; hence his character was one lived orderly. Had he been possessor of a love of discord, it would not have been his lot to delight in law, but rather to delight in chaos. Now this is God's law in which he delights; hence his character must have been lived according to this law, for it is human to have joy only in that which appeals to us and finds a response from us. It is God's law that tells us about him. To delight in his law is to delight in receiving more light about his love and character and way. We want to learn more about the person we love, and this yearning for knowledge is constant; for, "In His law doeth he meditate day and night."

* * * * * * * *

True manhood is blessed in its beauty. He is like a tree by rivers of water, bringing in fruit in season. Nothing in all the realm of nature is more attractive than a tree with its green leaves and outstretching branches. Pope said, "A tree is a nobler thing than a king in his coronation robes." "The groves were God's first temples."

We can see here the beauty of purpose. He shall be like a tree *planted* by the rivers of water. It did not simply happen so. A good man's character shows purpose and ideal. He has an aim, thought no one may know what it is, save the person possessing it.

We see here the beauty of good cheer and joy, "for his leaf shall not wither." His is an evergreen life. Others about him may be blackened by the snows of winter, but not so with him. When the snows of winter fall and try to freeze, even then his leaf shall not wither.

We also see the beauty of dependability. His fruit is of the right sort and in due season. The genuine character can be depended on at all times. The story is told of a recent investigation of Appalachian surveys. It is said that the surveys made by Washington years ago have shown themselves to be correct. What a record of faithful, honest service!

****

True manhood is blessed in earthly immortality. Of course it is also blessed in heavenly immortality, but we are prone to talk all the time about heavenly immortality, and forget earthly immortality. To be remembered in a right way after we go, is no little matter. Men have risked their lives, endured hardships, and even spent kingdoms, to have an earthly immortality. The way to get it is not by erecting pyramids, as did ancient Pharaohs; this did not perpetuate their lives. Moses never erected a pyramid, but today he is known better than any Pharaoh. He received an earthly immortality by acquiring genuine character. He shall be like a tree. A tree is planted by one generation and seen, admired and used by many following generations. So that is the way with one possessed of genuine manhood.

Some literary folks can perpetuate their memory by writing books, and some artistic people can leave their lives on earth by painting pictures. We cannot do this since we are not gifted in this way, but never-the-less we can leave our stamp here just the same; we do it by living as we should. We see many have handed over their lives to succeeding generations. The loudest voices in nearly every walk of life are the voices of the persons who are dead. Washington speaks in words that are heeded in halls of legislation. His voice is thus heeded, not because he climbed higher than his playmates and carved his name on the Natural Bridge in Virginia; his words are heeded because his character was like a tree planted by rivers of water. This is true of anything. Greece died, but Greek culture lives on. Rome died, but Roman law is still living and will continue to live. Jerusalem passed out, but Jerusalem religion will never leave us.

The reason this hero of ours, this man who has genuine character, will have an earthly immortality, is because he has an unfailing source to his character. He is planted by the river of water. God is the giver of real manhood. That manhood shall not perish from the earth as long as our Father lives.

A tree is a thing planted and grown. You cannot build a tree, nor can you build a character. Have it planted by faith in Jesus, and have it grown because planted by the rivers of water of God's grace. Rot. H. Adams had this poem in the Youth's Companion:

> *"Who plants a tree*
> *Plants not what is, but is to be--*
> *A hope, a thought for future years,*
> *A prayer, a dream of higher things*
> *That rise from out our doubts and fears,*
> *As seed or acorn, from the cold*
> *And dungeon darkness of the mold,*
> *To lights upsprings.*
>
> *"Who plants a tree*
> *Blesses earth's children yet to be,*
> *Toilers shall rest beneath its shade,*
> *The dreamers dream of golden hours,*
> *And frolic youth and winsome maid*

Shall bless the shadow that it gives;
So, happy birds among its leaves,
    And lowly flowers.

"Who plants a tree
Plants beauty where all eyes may see,
  In mirror of her loveliness,
    How Nature fashions beauteous forms
  Through sunny calms and darksome stress--
A parable of human life
 That grows to excellence through strife
    Of beating storms."

That Blessed Mother

And the angel came in unto her, and said, Hail, thou that art highly favored, the Lord is with thee: blessed art thou among women, *** For behold from henceforth all generations shall call me blessed (Luke 1:28, 48).

Chapter XI

The Beatific Verity On Motherhood.

As ships enter the harbor of our metropolis, the first object that arrests the attention of the incoming population on human-laden vessels, is the Statue of Liberty. This is a symbol of the liberty we enjoy and of a universal welcome to others who seek this liberty. The storms of the out-stretching ocean have not cooled the welcome, and the rains of years have not weakened it in the least. This welcome is to all who enter. This is but parabolic of a verity that is seen in all peoples, and through all times, the verity on true motherhood. Proverbs of all nations and songs of all climes have made her very name sacred to the human heart. This will always be so. True motherhood is one of the durable things of life that will be here after the sifting.

True motherhood, and honor and love to such, will abide because of three things: universal appreciation of mother, birth of the Son of God from an earthly mother, and the crowning of maternity which the Christian religion bestows. Christ and his religion tuned the Christian message to a universal and eternal note when pure motherhood was enthroned in Christian principle.

"By their fruits ye shall know them," is a rule applicable to all institutions, nations, classes, and individuals. This can be applied to mothers of men. The ideal mother is the one who, all things considered, mothers the ideal son. The greatest mother is the mother of the greatest son. The greatest son is the one who does the greatest good in the world. Christ was the greatest person who ever lived. His mother was the one mother who gave birth to an ideal human being, and the very God Incarnate

No wonder, in the first chapter of Luke, we read three verses honoring her: "and the angel came in unto her, and said, Hail thou that art highly favored, the Lord is with thee; blessed art thou among women (verse 28). and Elizabeth said, in verse 42: "Blessed art thou among women, and blessed is the fruit of thy womb." In verse 48 taken from Mary's song: "For from henceforth all generations shall call me blessed." She occupies a peculiar place among mothers and in Christian thought.

There are a great many things we do not know about Mary, and this ignorance is not an accident. We do not know where she was born, when she died, or where she was buried. Human imagination has tried to speak in a great many places where inspiration is silent, but human fancy and tradition can be of but little worth to us in this matter.

But while we do not accept so many fancied things about her life, yet she was a good woman. Evidently God did not expect for her to be worshiped, or he would have told us more about her. He has, it seems, hidden her tomb to keep devotees with more devotion than brains from making pilgrimages to it. Like Moses, her place in the world as just a human being, might have led to idolatry with respect to her tomb. So he secretly, as far as we are concerned, laid her away. It looks to me as if both Catholics and Protestants have made errors with respect to her character and life: the one regarding her as more than human, and the other not giving her the respect and admiration due her, our lack of appreciation being caused by our being afraid to accept some things as held by

Catholics. Now she is the world's one ideal mother, because she gave the world its one ideal son. She was chosen above all women in all ages through whom God was to come to humanity. This choice was not an accident or an arbitrary choice of God; she was chosen for fitness. Men choose friends, companions, and workmen because of fitness. God uses wisdom in his choice. He chose Paul because of his fitness, and Peter because of his fitness, and Abraham because of his fitness. She had found favor in God's sight, not because of any little whim on God's part, but because of Mary's piety and deep religious life. Now she has no intercessory power, and should not be prayed to, but she is the world's ideal mother, because she found favor with God. Maternity which finds favor with God is an eternal Gibraltar that storms and tempests shall not move.

She was blessed in meditation. There are so many things Mary knew, but did not tell to the world. We are anxious to know how he talked when he was a child learning to shape words, and how he learned to walk, and what he said to his brothers and sisters, and little playfellows; but a deep and unbroken silence is the only reply we receive for our desire to reverently know these things. Luke received his information from Mary with reference to those first chapters in his book, but what she did not tell would make a library. She just kept these things and pondered them in her heart. She, that mother, made her life a rocky coast against which the great sea waves struck with force and sound. We, back on the shore, only receive the mist and dew and rain. That great meditative heart must hold all, and those lips must only express what we need to know. So, universally, the maternal privilege of silence and meditation is a dear one. It gives dignity, quiet, and poise.

> "Boy, your mother's dreaming,
> There's a picture fair and bright,
> That gladdens all her gracious tasks,
> At morning, noon, and night."

Let her dream on, and God bless her. Let her mediate and ponder in her heart.

She was blessed in humiliation and sacrifice Mary must have been misunderstood in the position she occupied. Her character of the highest type must have been maligned, though nothing is said to that effect in the Gospels. God was with her, in that her husband knew and understood, but before he learned the secret, he had planned to secretly put her away.

In this she was an ideal mother; not that such are maligned and misunderstood, but that all are called on to suffer. The greatest sufferers are the mothers. When husbands and sons step from the paths of rectitude and honor, and begin to go down into the sad depths of sin and disgrace, they suffer some, but the greatest sufferers, even in this case, are the mothers and wives. When hellish war, the last of the uncivilized institutions to die, demands our men and boys to feed it, they go like heroes and bleed and die. But the greatest sufferers even then are the blessed mothers. It seems to have been the general law of God, though unwritten, that the mothers were to be the world's greatest sufferers. But perfection is through suffering.

She was blessed in appreciation and love. No one will appreciate an effort as much as will a mother, and no love will overlook a fault as will her love. We are taught that when they saw Moses was a proper child, they hid him away. All children are proper children to mothers. I think the mother of Moses planned that little boat and lined it with a mother's love. I think she tested the strength of its side with the strength of her hope and heart. She must have floated it in the tears of a broken heart before she sent it out into the Nile. The father may have foresight and outlook, but insights belongs to the mother. She it is who loves the most and shows the most appreciation.

She was also blessed in hope and anticipation. No wonder Mary said to the servants in Cana in Galilee, "Whatsoever he saith unto you, do it." She was expecting to see him perform a miracle, though she had never seen one from his hand. This passage forever silences the legendary stories about his boyhood miracle, for it was spoken of by John as the first. But though she had never seen a miracle from him, yet she fully expected one, and did not hesitate to show this expectation. This is but typical of her whole life, which was lived in hope and in the joy of anticipation. But all mothers do the same; as they look at the child at play, they fancy they can see the man at work. As they hear the baby prattle about the house, they fancy this prattle is the eloquence of manhood in halls of law and legislation. Let them hope on; these hopes are the guiding stars of life!

She was blessed in inspiration and influence. Just how much Mary had to do with the childhood and manhood of the Savior, we shall never know. He, as a boy, watched her knead her bread, and saw how leaven worked. He followed her to the market place and learned its lessons. He learned how a poor woman will sweep the whole house to find a lost coin, and how a wise woman does not put new patches on old garments.

Her songs must have been a constant inspiration to him. Any mother sings a song to sooth and inspire. A rich man sat by the side of a friend and listened to the world's greatest soprano voice; they were both in tears. The friend spoke and asked this question: "Is that not the greatest singing you ever heard?" To his surprise the answer came, "No." "Who did you ever hear that could beat it?" "I have heard three songs," said the rich man, "that surpassed this one. The first was the song sung by my mother to me when I was a small boy. The other, a song by my wife, a song of love that came floating through the window when we were first married: and the last one was when my little tottling boy, now grown to manhood, was sung to sleep by his mother." But what songs the savior must have heard! His mother, in her song, as given in Luke proves herself to be a remarkable woman. The wild lyrics of an Oriental tribe were in her soul, and she had heard angel choruses. She may have repeated snatches from these angel songs to sooth the troubled heart of her child. Her whole life was to him an inspiration. A young man in Massachusetts came near drowning, but saved his life by swimming a mile. When his mother asked him how he did it, he answered: "I thought of you, mother, and kept on swimming."

God bless our mothers and their memories. Give them the best there is in this life, and in the life that is to come, the place they rightly deserve.

Slightly changing the words of a not-to-familiar poem:

> *"I hope there will be a sunset golden,*
>   *When she bids the world goodnight;*
> *I hope there will be no leaden sky*
>   *For clouding her failing sight.*
> *I want her to sail down the crimson West,*
> *When the ocean rocks the sun to rest,*
> *And the stars shine out on eve's fair breast,*
>   *When she bids the world goodnight.*
>
> *"I hope they will surge a flood of song*

To drive away every fear;
A crooning breeze through the listening trees.
When the twilight draweth near.
And I want her to hear the nesting bird,
And the tinkling bells of the homing herd;
A soothing voice and a tender word.
When she bids the world goodnight."

The Magnitude Of The Miniature

And he took a child and set him in the midst of them: and when he had taken him in his arms, he said unto them, Whosoever shall receive on of such children in my name, receiveth me: and whosoever receiveth me, receiveth not me, but him that sent me (Mark 9:36, 37).

And he took them in his arms, put his hands on them and blessed them (Mark 10:16).

Chapter XII

The Beatific Verity On Childhood.

A little child has been placed by the hands of Christ into the midst of the shifting, changing ages, and shall never be removed. The interest of the world today, as never before, is centering around our children, and this is not accidental. The primary reason for this lively and cumulative interest in childhood, is the touch of our Savior on the children. Christ and his Gospel message have helped most powerfully to bring the appreciation of the children to the place it now occupies. There are many of the plain folk of life who love the children; all of the really great folk of life have loved the children. Since the day our Savior took children into his arms and blessed them, it seems to have become an unwritten law that all really great people must appreciate the beauties and wonders of childhood.

If one has not pursued literature with this especially in mind, he has absolutely no idea how much of our best writing are devoted to appreciative remarks about childhood. If one has not read biography with this alone in view, he will never understand how most of our best men and women have numbered little children as their truest friends.

Victor Hugo was the great poet of France, and he has become universally famous for his love of children. Our own poets, in writing verses of appreciation of his greatness, have in many places referred to his love of childhood.

Longfellow used to invite the children to his home and play with them as though he were himself a little child. On his seventy-second birthday they presented him with a chair made from the spreading chestnut tree referred to in his poem, "The Village Blacksmith." These are his lines to children:

> *"What the leaves are to the forest,*
> *With light and air for food,*
> *Ere their sweet and tender juices*
> *Have been hardened into wood:*
>
> *"That, to the world are children:*
> *Through them it feels the glow*
> *Of a brighter and sunnier climate*
> *Than reaches the trunks below."*

James Whitcome Riley said of Longfellow:

> *"Though he knew the tongues of nations,*
> *And their meanings all are dear,*
> *The prattle and lisp of a little child*
> *Was the sweetest for him to hear."*

William Ellery Channing, the first and by far the greatest Unitarian, said in his symphony, among other great things: "To listen to stars and birds, babes and sages with open heart, this is to be my symphony."

It is said that Emerson preferred the company of a child to a conversation with a philosopher. His reason for this preference was that he could, by being with a child, learn more of the real things of life.

Some of the best touches in the poems of Whittier are when he refers to child life, whether he be talking about "the school house by the road, a ragged beggar standing," or "the barefoot boy with cheek of tan."

In the life of Julia Ward Howe, by her daughters, reference is made to the frequent visits of Edwin Booth to her home. On one of these occasions Mrs Howe invited to her home many of the noted of Beacon Street. After the briefest and shyest greetings, the actor, who was world-famed, retired to the corner of the room and began making dolls and rabbits out of pocket handkerchief for eight-year-old Maude.

Hood's lines are familiar:

"I remember, I remember,
The fir trees dark and high
I used to think their slender tops
Were close against the sky.

"It was a childish ignorance,
But now 'tis little joy
To know I'm farther off from heaven
Than when I was a boy."

Wordsworth said: "Heaven lies about us in our infancy."

There are many instances in the life of Beecher which bring out this love from his great heart. The homes of his members where he visited were generally the homes where there were children, and he was a special favorite with them. They always felt a sharp disappointment if they, by being absent, could not hear his stories and see his smiles. He, on such occasions, felt the same disappointment. The incident told by the Rev. C. Hall, in his funeral oration over Mr. Beecher, is illustrative of his whole life. The last Sunday evening he preached in the church, after the congregation had nearly all gone and only a few remained to practice some music, some street urchins dropped in, attracted by the music, when they saw Mr. Beecher watching them, they feared he would drive them out, but instead he had the organist play some sweet music for them, and after this put his arms around them and walked home with them.

But why all this appreciation, and much more I might mention of Dickens, Scott, Burns, Goldsmith, Lowell, Riley, Fields, Edmund Vance Cook, and hundreds of others? Simply to enforce the statements found in Mark 9:36,37:" And he took a child and set him in the midst of them; and when he had taken him in his arms, he said unto them, Whosoever shall receive one of such children in my name, receiveth me: and whosoever shall receive me, receiveth not me, but him that sent me;" and also in Mark 10: 16:"And he took them up in his arms, put his hands upon them and blessed them."

The children had that about them which attracted our Savior as none before him had been attracted. He placed the child in the center, not only of the disciples, but of the whole world, and he has been in the center ever since, in the thinking of the good and the really great. Furthermore, if the child were really put in the center of the thoughts of all as he is in the thoughts of the noble and good, many of the social, national, and even international problems would be solved.

These two passages of scripture are quoted much, but not too much. The one arose from a debate among the ambitious disciples, as to who should be the greatest one among them. The other came from the bringing by the mothers of their babes to 'Christ. The one came from an evil thought, and the other from a holy one. But regardless of this, Christ makes both incidents redound to the glory of God and to the glory of childhood. Whose child he placed in the midst of the disciples has long since ceased to be a matter of debate, for no one knows. Tradition tells us that this boy was Ignatius the Martyr, who later became pastor in Antioch. This is very uncertain, to say the least. It was probably in the home of Peter, and may have been his boy. This, too, is uncertain. Get the picture of the Savior preaching and the child being interested enough to be near him and to be taken into his arms. I do not think the children objected to being taken by our Savior. They have some way of knowing the person to whom to go.

Since that time, when children have been born into the world, we have gone back in mind to the mystic land of dreams where life is eternal and God is king. Christ gave more than these mothers asked when they brought their children. They asked that the children be touched by his hand, but instead he took them into his arms.

This beatific verity of his on childhood, like the beatitudes of the Sermon on the Mount, contradicts existing standards of morals and values. We can look into the contemporary thought of the Romans, Egyptians, Greeks, or any other people, and see how his words met a surging sea of opposition. First Century thought abhorred the idea of a strong man loving a little child. The same conceptions are held today by non-Christian peoples. Read Dan Crawford's "Thinking Black," and you will weep because of the mistreatment of children. "Childhood in the Mohammedan World," by Zwemer, also shows the difference between the children of Christians and of non-Christians.

Why, the disciples even did not know what Jesus thought of children. They objected to the mothers bringing their children to Jesus. Christ has always had a hard time making his disciples think his thoughts, instead of thinking the thoughts of the world and then assuming they are his. His followers try to do that, even now, about war and many other things.

I think our Savior saw all the past in the child and, for that reason, placed him in the center of appreciation. He blessed him, because in him he saw the past ages of history unfold. This child had life, and Christ loved life. He had the life of all the past, and Christ saw that. Whether you understand all the power of heredity or not, matters little just now, in our discussion; but you must surely see that the race is repeated in the life of every individual person. Just as the lump of coal is giving forth the heat of centuries gone by so the unfolding life of the child is revealing to us, in miniature, the race of man, physically, mentally, and morally,

Not only did our Savior recognize what the relation was between the past of the human race and the child, but he also saw what the relation of the present was to the child. The child has much more intelligence than we think. Parents who object to their children becoming Christians at an early age, manifest a criminal ignorance of child life.

The example of the child as it lives the Christ life is quite forceful; and in hundreds of instances we see illustrated the statement, "A little child shall lead them." The ruffian in Moore's Lalla Rookh let fall from his eye the tear of repentance, by means of which heaven's gate was opened, simply because he saw a child kneeling in prayer.

Christ also saw great possibilities of the future in children. If you touch the child life of today, you have influenced tomorrow. Satan sees this, as we learn from the plans of saloons. They try to create appetite for drink in boys, so they will have drinkers and drunkards tomorrow. We must, like our Savior, see the oak tree in the acorn, the bird in the songless egg, and the man in the playful child. The child is the father of the man.

We should make our lives, as grown folks, just as attractive to the children as possible. We should make our religion just as inviting to them as possible. A mother on one occasion saw her child backing off a high cliff. She was afraid to call, in fright, lest the child tumble over; so she simply opened her arms and smiled, and the little child rushed into her welcoming embrace. We must make our religion thus.

Again it becomes us as parents always to remember we are being watched and followed. A Persian king was returning home from a hunt. A courier announced to him that a garden full of ripened fruit had been found. His followers begged him to partake, but her refused. He gave as his reason, "others will follow my example, and as a result no fruit will be left for the owner.

"If my child is just like me,
   What kind of a child will my child be?"

A Bright Light In A Dark Picture

Blessed is he whose transgression is forgiven, whose sin is covered. Blessed is the man unto who the Lord imputeth not iniquity, and in whose spirit there is no guile (Psalms 32:1, 2).

Chapter XIII

The Beatific Verity On The Forgiven.

I saw an artist color an interesting picture in the presence of an audience. It was the picture of a house in darkness; not one bit of cheer was suggested to the audience. It was a house in a dark wood, with sombre complaining trees for a background, and with snow covering the whole surface of the scene. Then after he had panted his picture and had spoken of the uninviting aspect of it all, he said: "But there is a bright light in this dark picture." With one stroke of the brush, he threw into the picture a light in the window. It changed the picture of the landscape and brightened up the whole horizon. Not a feeling of sadness, but instead, a feeling of good cheer was sent through the interested audience.

We can see this repeated in the religious experience of forgiven man. In Psalms 32: 1-2, we read of such a picture: "Blessed is he whose transgression is forgiven, whose sin is covered. Blessed is the man unto whom the Lord imputeth not iniquity, and in whose spirit there is no guile." In this passage the Psalmist begins his picture with the bright light in it, but he hastens in the next breath to tell us of the time when it was not there, and of how dark and sombre was the picture before the bright light was placed on it. The dark picture is a man without forgiveness, and the bright picture is a man standing in possession of it.

This passage of scripture has proven itself to be very helpful to many of the good people of the world. Dr. Maclaren speaks of it as a leaf from the autobiography of David. It is generally conceded that this is a Dividic Psalm, and it also must be conceded that the language is too vivid to refer to any save the king himself. Paul however, makes a universal application of these words; they then refer to all people. When Luther was asked which of the psalms he liked the best, he answered the Pauline Psalms, and this one he included in that list. Augustine used to read this passage weeping, and he had it printed above his death bed, that he might see it often and meditate on its meaning to his own life and experience.

There are just two pictures here, the dark picture and the dark picture with a bright light in it.

****

The dark picture is a portrait of a man in his sins without forgiveness. This uninviting picture must be seen and fully appreciated if we are to understand all the beauty of the second picture. As we look at this black picture, we cannot help but see what sin is to a life.

We must see sin in its universality. I suppose David was referring to some particular moment in his life, but Paul makes a universal application of his remarks. Any remark about sin can be made to have a universal application without impairing its meaning. This is true because sin is universal. All races have sinned, and strange to say, all races have committed the same sins. A missionary was reading the first two chapters of Romans to an audience of Chinamen, and they become enraged. On asking the reason, they said: "You are talking about us." He informed them that this was written hundreds of years ago, but they said: "No, you have written it since you came over here."

Not only do we see that sin is universal, but we see it is universally recognized. All races have seen their own sin and have tried to get rid of it in some way. The laws of all lands show this, and the very basest of heathen religions deal with sin as a fact.

We can also see, by a close study of this passage, that sin, as far as each individual is concerned, is a result of man's volition. He has the ability to sin. This means much. The big wheel in a machine has not the ability to keep from going around in the way it does. The bird has not the ability to keep from singing as it does. But man has personality, intelligence, power and freedom. These are necessary if he is to have the ability to sin.

We can also see sin in its nature brought forth in this passage. There are four words used for sin in our text. To transgress, means to step over a line. To sin, means to miss the mark. Iniquity means to turn out of a proper channel. Fraud means to give the wrong impression. Each one implies a perfect standard, and they all bring to our mind the fact that this perfect standard has not been lived up to. It shows that the person has not been living on schedule time. It may be natural for man to sin now, but it was not so at the first. He was not made physically, mentally, morally, or spiritually to sin; he was made to be perfect. That is why God condemns sin; he knows it is best for man not to sin. It is silly to get angry with God for telling you to get out of a burning house; he did not set it on fire. He is telling you to get out for your own benefit, not to show his knowledge of the fire or his ability to convey this information to you. If there were no God, no heaven, no hell nor any institution now in existence because of these, sin would still be sin and still be hurtful to the race. And furthermore, not only would sin still be hurtful, but there would still be sin. Sin is everywhere, and shows up bad everywhere. It is a violation of the laws of our being and must bring results as such. If I violate a law in the circulation of blood through the body, by cutting a blood vessel, then I must suffer as a result. If I violate the laws of the piano by pounding on the keys with a hammer, I should certainly work an injury to the piano; it was not constructed for such use. Burrowing animals which violate the laws of their nature by living under the earth, have been punished with blindness. The little mules in the mines of Australia are blind because of their remaining out of the light so long. Thus we can see the nature and the results of sin in a life.

* * * * * * * * *

All of these things blacken the picture and make us long for the light to dawn. When it dawns, such joy it brings that David shouts: "Blessed." to appreciate all the brightness of this picture after the light has been put into it, we must fully appreciate the difficulty of putting the light in the picture. We must see that forgiveness of sin is no little or easy task. It is so hard that none can forgive sins, save God only. It is too big a task for any man. Plato thought nature could not forgive, and therefore he doubted if God could. At the time of the healing of the man borne of four, we see the crowd wonder at Jesus forgiving the man's sin, and they make the statement that only God can do this. Christ seems to admit the truth of their statement, but goes on to prove by his miracle of healing that he can forgive sins because he is God. Things, however, which are impossible for man to do, are possible for God. Our Bible tells us God can do it. We ourselves say so when we imperfectly forgive men their wrongs against us. Our very hopes say so.

But what does it mean to forgive sin? It means to have the past blotted out. The figure here of having sin covered, goes back to the dim past for its origin. It refers to the ancient way of writing on wax tablets. When one tablet was filled, then it must be re-waxed, and it is new again. You can thus easily see the character effects of forgiveness. A man disgusted with himself and all concerned, is ready to quit trying to be a man, but now he is forgiven; his life is re-waxed, and he has a new start. Optimism takes the place of pessimism, and hope takes the lead of despair. He now is in position to pray to God without ceasing. Before this he was bashful in God's presence. He has now free access to the throne of grace. "Blessed is the man to whom the Lord imputeth not iniquity." this is a forensic term.

The beauty of it appears on the surface. When one feels the awful pangs of sin, and then has he relations re-established with God by forgiveness, not wonder he thinks himself blessed. Spurgeon refers to this passage as bundles of blessedness. The plural is used her that emphasis may be put on the joy of forgiveness.

* * * * * * * * * * *

Is there any cost connected with the changing of a dark picture into a bright one? Yes, a very dear one; it has a two-fold cost: a Godward cost and a manward cost; it cost God Calvary. I am not prepared here to give my theory of atonement; it is very unsatisfactory to me, and like all other theories of atonement will prove unsatisfactory to you. We care not for theories on this question, but for facts. We all know and admit that the death of Jesus Christ has something to do with the forgiveness of sins. We know without this atonement God could not forgive sins; we know this forgiveness is necessary for man to be happy, and that the death of our Savior was God's greatest price. It may seem cheap to you, but it is very costly, indeed.

Not only do we see the cost of a cross on the one side, but we see a similar cost on the other side. It costs the individual forgiven also a cross. He is told that if he enjoys the forgiveness God can give through the Cross of Christ, he must have a cross also. A cross he must have, not crosses. Now yours is a cross of repentance. This cross of repentance implies conviction, confession, renunciation, pledge to loyalty, and many other things. But this is necessary; God cannot forgive an unrepentant soul. When the Psalmist kept silence he had no peace; he had no forgiveness. If you pay your cost in it, God will forgive your iniquity, and in the dark picture of your life, a bright light will shine forth.

A Universal God.

Blessed is the nation whose God is the Lord: and the people whom he hath chosen for his own inheritance (Psalms33:12).

Chapter XIV.

The Beatific Verity On The Religious Nation.

Is there such a thing in the world as a religious nation? In the strictest sense, there is not such a thing. If we use the words loosely, there may be such a thing as a religious nation. When the Supreme Court of the United States said this was a Christian country, they used the terms in a very loose and general way. In the strictest sense, to be a Christian means to be born again; to be regenerated and given a new nature. Now the only thing which can be born again is an individual; a nation cannot be born again , nor can a home, a city, an age, or any other group. Not only is regeneration confined to individuals, but to individuals who are old enough and wise enough to believe.

For a man or a group of men to name a nation a Christian nation, does not make it so at all. Naming is not naturing. Some of the most unchristian nations on earth have been called Christian nations. They are neither Christian in ideal or in fact. Giving a country a state religion and making that state religion the Christian religion, is not making the nation Christian. The most Christian nation under the sun has no state religion.

To make a nation a Christian nation in the general sense- and that is the only way we can make a Christian country- is to so teach the spirit of Christ that men are influenced by it in their lives. The way to make a home Christian is to lead a sufficient number of the members of the home to Christ that the ideal and standards of the home shall be Christian ideals and standards. Laws and customs in any country are controlled by public sentiment. This public sentiment is shaped by the individuals making up the population of the country. If you can reach a sufficient number of these persons in any government with the Gospel and, in turn, have them shape and determine the public sentiment of the country, so that in the end the ideals, customs, and laws shall be shaped, you have made a Christian country. Christianity has always concerned itself with individuals and expects them, in turn, to lead to general ideals and standards. It is a Christian nation, then, whose public policy is that of mercy and justice, and whose word is taken away from home, nothing doubting. It is a Christian government when weaker nations are not afraid of being cheated by it, because the home affairs of such a nation are governed by statesmen and not politicians. It is a nation whose home affairs are open and honest, and whose citizenship is made up of industrious and fair men. It is a Christian nation when it regards a man's life as being worth more than the life of a sheep, and a home as being of more value than many millions of capital stock. This is a Christian nation. Such a nation is indeed a blessed nation.

* * * * * * * * * * * * *

Nor is this an idle dream, for nations can possess such ideals and standards. This possibility is shown plainly from the text. This verse would never have been written had this been an impossible thing. What is possible for one nation is possible for all.

This is possible from the viewpoint of God. God can save a sufficient number of individuals in any nation to determine the home and foreign policies of that nation. He made all nations. He has beautified all nations. He has made the cherry blossoms of Japan to be as beautiful as the roses of our own Southland. He has made the Alps and the Rockies alike majestic. He has made the waters of the Nile as well as the waters of the Jordan or the Mississippi. He is the God of all nations, and not of one only. He has created all men, as well as those of one race, in his own image. All nations are made of one blood. He tells us in his Word to ask of him and have the nations for an inheritance. He has also said that the knowledge of the Lord shall cover the earth, as the waters cover the sea. From the viewpoint of God in his plans and hopes and powers, this is a possibility.

This is a possibility from the viewpoint of man. Individuals from all nations are capable of being Christians of the most consecrated type. Nobody with average intelligence doubts this. To doubt this and to confess such a doubt, is an open confession of consummate ignorance. Not only do we see these individuals as being capable of being Christians , but we see them as being willing to be Christians. This is very vividly shown by Mr. Sherwood Eddy"s report of his preaching tour abroad. Among the cities visited by him were Manila, Calcutta, Constantinople, Tonio, and Peking. In Peking he was met by the man who was then President of the Chinese Republic, who manifested an interest in his work. He was invited to luncheon by the Vice President of the nation, who gave him an audience to which to speak. Composed of his family and friends. The Minister of the Interior granted him a site for his pavilion, which site was in front of the Imperial Palace. The Minister of War gave him the loan of two hundred war tents to cover the pavilion and make it rain -proof. The Minister of Education gave a half holiday to all the Government students, that they might attend his meetings. Four thousand university students heard his first message. On the third night there were one thousand inquirers. Fourteen thousand heard his messages in Peking, and twelve newspapers gave wider publicity to them. These same papers, after he went away, carried articles on Christianity. Bible classes were organized for all who might want to learn more, and two hundred young Chinese gentleman were teachers of these classes. This is but one city in the big world, but a city we generally supposed the hardest to reach. Space would fail us to speak of the reception given the Good News in all lands. Instead of cramming the Gospel down the throats of people who do not want it, we are answering the call, "Come over and help."

* * * * * * * * * *

Not only do we see that it is possible to make all nations Christian nations, but we can see that it is exceedingly profitable. Godliness is indeed profitable for both lives, this present one and the future life also. It is as profitable for one nation as it is for another, for the God who makes possible this godliness has made all nations able to receive it. I do not like the term, " foreign missions", I like the term, " world-wide missions", much better. There are no foreign missions in the Twentieth Century. The world is so small, with our many inventions, and the seas so narrow, with our improved ways of travel, that the nations we used to term foreign nations now occupy the place of near neighbors. What the Gospel does for Texas or New York, it also does for China or India. There is no soil where the Rose of Sharon does not bloom in beauty. There is a material advantage in the Gospel.

When John G. Paton went to the New Hebrides Islands, it is said the ships would not land on the shores for trading purposes; the sailors feared lest poison arrows would be sent into their bodies. After he had taught the Gospel and led these persons to Christ, the islands were opened up to foreign trade. Of course, this is the lowest reason possible for the spread of Christianity, nevertheless, a reason, and a sufficient on to cause us to say, "Blessed is the nation whose God is the Lord."

We also see the profit of good wholesome laws being framed as a result of the spread of the Gospel. An English jurist dreamed a dream in which he saw all the laws inspired by the Bible and Christian teaching torn from his law books. When he awoke he looked into his books to see just what would have happened had this been the case, and, according to his statement, one-third of every page would have been removed and the other two-thirds left meaningless. Our laws of sanitation and home protection, our laws of education and public decency, all come from men who are inspired with the Christian ideals.

We can also see the profit of educational progress and spread of intelligence in any nation as a result of Christian teaching. The old stall system of China began to give way to new and scientific universities, in proportion to the acceptance of the missionaries' message of Jesus. While Christianity is not education, its spread has always increased educational institutions of the best class. In many of the Government schools of China and Japan, the teachers are Christian in ideal, character, and profession. Had it not been for the Christian message, there would be no State schools in this country, or Government schools in a foreign country, which would be worth attending. Go to the heathen countries and study their school system, where they have any, or to a Mohammedan country, and study their school life, and you will see the truthfulness of my statement.

We can see the profit of moral reform and clean living as a result of the spread of the Gospel. Immoral practices and institutions go in proportion to the coming of Christ. The Christian message struck the chains off the hands of slaves. The Gospel of Jesus is driving the saloon, the gambling den, and the brothel from our land. As it drives these things from our land, it drives opium smoking from China and the drinking of the waters of Ganges River from India. It has done much toward removing the injurious habit of foot binding from China.

The spirit of charity and the desire to relieve human suffering are to be seen as profitable in any country. These come from the spread of the Gospel. The brigade of nurses and skilled doctors, the company of charity workers, the many agencies for feeding the poor and caring for the sick—these all come from Jesus and his message.

These are the indirect results of Christ and his message, and these he has made secondary to the real profit of Christianity. The first thing he proposes to do, and the most important thing he can do, is to make a man like God by regeneration, and thus prepare him to live and also to die. This can be done only through the spread of the spirit and Gospel of Jesus.

****

Now how can those things be? Not by an edict or a court or council making in a day a nation nominally Christian. This is not the method of our Christ. It can be done by one individual touching another, and this other touching still another, until the knowledge of our God shall cover the earth as the waters cover the sea.

The Moral Discipline Of Temptation.

Blessed is the man who endureth temptation: for when he is tried, he shall receive the crown of life, which the Lord hath promised to them that love him. Let no man say when he is tempted, I am tempted of God: for God cannot be tempted of evil, neither tempteth he any man: but every man is tempted when he is drawn away of his own lust, and enticed (James 1:12-14).

Chapter XV.

The Beatific Verity On The Approved.

We are told that the tree from which our ancestors were told not to eat was in the center of the original garden. This is not an accident. It was in the center of the garden where all walks met, and where the children of men were most apt to be. It was the most frequented spot in the garden. So it is today; temptations are where the race goes by. All races, and all individuals in every race, have passed by this forbidden tree. Job, Abraham, Joseph, Jacob, David, Peter, John, Paul, Socrates, Plato, Homer, Caesar, Cromwell, and all others have felt the touch of temptation in their lives. When we seek some things that must be reckoned with in all ages, we do well not to overlook temptations and how to meet them. They are about the same in reality in all ages, though they may take different forms according to the circumstances of the occasion.

We do well to study closely the nature of temptation, that we may be able to see some things which are determined as a natural result. James tells us in the text that a man is tempted when he is drawn away of his own lusts and enticed. Then, temptation is a "drawing away." The word is here used which means to entice fishes from their hiding place under the rock; bait is used, and the fish is drawn away from his place of safety. So we are not tempted to be thieves, but to step from the path of honesty; not to be libertines, but to step from the path of virtue; not to be drunkards, but to step from the path of soberness.

With this idea of temptation in mind, we can plainly see that a temptation is a failure or a success according as it finds a response in our heart and life. It amounts to nothing, unless it finds an ally on the inside of our lives to assist and encourage it. Our Christ was tempted in the wilderness to digress from proper paths, but these temptations were fruitless because they found nothing in his soul and life which responded to the drawing away.

With this idea of temptation we can also see something as to the origin of wrong doing. God does not send evil into the world, nor does he want it to be in the world. He does send those things which are quite often converted into that which is wrong. He sends circumstances from which temptations arise. He did not send the temptations, for God cannot be tempted of evil, neither tempteth he any man. What he means to try us, or test us, or prove us, may be turned by the devil in us into temptations. God's testing is to bring out and develop character while Satan can change the occasion of character-development into character-destruction. God's purpose is to give a probation, while the devil makes the probation into a temptation. Many of the good things of life have been converted into evil purposes. Corn was made for food, that with it people might be kept from starvation. Satan makes it into poison, that with it people might be intoxicated and finally brought to starvation. You send your child to town with a dollar, and your purpose is to discipline your child in trading and thus teach him the worth of money. But on the way an evil companion is met and the child is enticed to spend the money for something useless and perhaps harmful. In this instance, are you the author of temptation? I tell you, nay. Your purpose was a holy one, but the child has been drawn away.

Now there are perhaps two kinds of temptations, roughly speaking: the new ones and the old ones. The new ones have their origin in the taking for a wrong purpose that which was meant for good. The old ones are largely responsible to past conduct for their origin. Your life yesterday determines your temptations today. Your manner of meeting temptations today determines your temptations tomorrow. Old temptations are in a way penal. You can make old temptations impossible by not yielding to new ones.

By thus seeing the nature of temptation we can also see the variety of its approach. It comes from every possible direction. It is hard to think of circumstances from which temptations may not come. Nearly everything containing possibilities for good also contains possibilities for evil.

There is a moral discipline in temptations when they are met in the right spirit and overcome in a triumphant manner. Every place in life is purchased with a price, and character is a sum total of victories won over temptations. Some people would read our text, "Blessed is the man who never had a temptation." These persons would most assuredly miss the meaning of James in our text. "Blessed is the man that endureth temptation." This is true because to be blessed means to be in possession of such happiness as the God of the universe has. To have that happiness, you must have a sense of power, and to have that sense of power, you must be a conquerer over sin. Browning said, "Then welcome each rebuff that turns earth's smoothness rough." Welcome these things, because they are the refining fires that bring out the true silver; they are the furnaces that bake the soft bits of clay into bricks.

"Obstacles are things to be overcome," said Napoleon And we may add, as we overcome them, we are made strong and able. If temptations win, they break you. If you win, they make you. Watkinson tells us of a Russian general who captured an enemy, emptied the magazine of the conquered, and from the lead received, made medals for his troops to wear. What was intended to destroy the lives of the Russian soldiers was worn by them as signs of triumph and victory. Why did the American Indian keep a record of the scalps he took, or the head-hunter of Borneo string the skulls of the people he had slain, or David carry to camp the foreskins of the Philistines he had taken in battle? For the simple reason that the superstitious supposed the strength of the conquered went into the conqueror.

Nor is such reasoning altogether wrong; every victory you win adds another bit of strength to your right arm of power. Gunsaulus said, "Let every man remember that masterful men, like their Master, are not devil-driven, but Spirit-driven to be tempted, not of the Spirit, but 'Of the devil!' The higher his destiny the more surely do the forces of goodness lift any man, born for mastery, up to a height which flings correspondingly vast shadows into the vale below."

There is also the discipline of a revelation of our own weakness. If a man did not have to pass by the tree of temptation in this life, he would begin to think himself like God and would be arrogant and haughty. His temptations keep him from being egotistic and from thinking himself, Achilles-like, invulnerable. As a natural result, from this realization of our weakness there comes a sympathy for others who are tempted, and we endeavor to bear one another's burdens.

We can also see that temptations teach us the source of all true victory. Temptations teach us the way to the throne of grace and how to incarnate the strength of God in our lives.

You an I are the keys to success or failure in our temptations. There are some things we may do to help God win the victory, or there are some things we can do that can keep him from winning the victory. Our continuous prayer should be, "Lead us not into temptation," and all our efforts should be to answer that prayer.

Another thing we should do which will help us in meeting life's testing time, is to realize that every kind of temptation has not only been met by Jesus, but by human beings also. No man has a peculiar temptation. Sometimes he thinks he has and thus expresses himself, but this is a mistake, for you have no temptation which is not common to man. If other human beings have conquered temptation, you may do it too.

Another thing that will help us in overcoming temptation, is to shun the very appearance of evil. Satan never goes too far at any time. He never tempts a man to be a drunkard, but to take just one more drink; not to be a thief, but to steal just a small piece of money. If we adopt the platform of shunning the very appearance of evil, we have largely solved the temptation problem.

Another thing that will be of great help to us in our temptations, is to know that God will help us and strengthen us for temptations when they come. He has all power in heaven and in earth, and he is willing to use this power for the protection and the keeping of his people. With every temptation there is a way to escape.

Life's Great Adventure.

Jesus saith unto him, Thomas, because thou hast seen me, thou hast believed: blessed are they that have not seen, and yet have believed *(John 20:19).*

Chapter XVI.

The Beatific Verity On Faith In The Unseen Christ.

Christians in all ages have spent much time discussing the subject of faith, and have made it rather hard to find out just what our Savior had in mind when he talked about it. When we drag any subject into the realm of theology and theological text-books, as a general thing, it will be so confused by theories given about it, as to be understood only with difficulty. A good rule to follow in studying any subject which has been much discussed, is to strip it of all that has been said about it and take the words of only Christ on the subject. Let us do this with the subject of faith.

This is the best passage in the Bible, illustrating our Savior's conception of faith. It gives us an occasion pregnant with meaning, and the real words of Jesus on this important subject. Thomas had been doubting the resurrection of Jesus from the dead, and had made the statement to the other disciples that he would not believe in the resurrection unless he saw the physical signs of suffering and crucifixion in Christ's living body. Jesus gives him his requests, and then gives our text in the form of a beatitude. That is what he means by faith-believing what we cannot see. The author of Hebrews-I do not know his name-gives about the same idea, "Faith is the substance of things hoped for, the evidence of things not seen." An old reading of this text is, "Faith is giving substance to unseen things, hoped for with evidence." Augustine asks the question, "What is faith, but believing what you do not see?" After all, that is why Abraham was called the father of the faithful. He believed what he could not see, took God at his word, and traveled toward a country which he had not seen. He indeed made life's great adventure.

Now one view of faith that finds some one to express it in nearly ever age, is that faith is the opposite to reason. If reason says one thing and God and faith say another, which will you accept? is their question? Well, our answer is that reason does not say an opposite thing to God; faith is not an antithesis to reason. It does not mean "receiving without perceiving" in any sphere. Faith and reason are inter-dependent. You cannot reason without faith, and you cannot have faith without reason. Faith is that which makes us accept the invisible, but on the ground of evidence and reason.

Dr. Ira Maclaren, in "the Mind of the Master," names faith as the sixth sense, and also calls it the religious instinct. Now it may be the sixth sense, but it is not an exclusive religious instinct. It is used and must be used in all forms of reasoning. It is that element in our mental make-up that makes the invisible seen. Beecher is right in his statement, "Faith, therefore, is not any one experience relating to religion alone, or to moral themes alone; it is a generic term, that designates the action of mind in certain relations toward invisible truths; and it is as large as the capacity of man; as large as the assignable universe; as large as the great outlying world bout us." We can thus see the exercise of faith and its work in the realm of discovery. New worlds came into being and were inhabited by peoples from old worlds, not because someone contradicted the rules of laws and reason, but because they reasoned a little closer than others had reasoned before, and then had a little more faith-enough to see the invisible. Now we see faith is a necessity to every discovery. In the realm of invention we are able to see the same necessity. The same is true of science. There is much more faith exercised in a scientific laboratory than is exercised in the average church house.

With this conception of faith, we can take up the text and apply it to our own heart-experiences. We may have many reasons for believing in and trusting the unseen Christ. He is a blind man who refuses to accept such evidence as we have. No jury would hesitate one moment in giving a verdict on the ground of such evidence. We have much stronger evidence for believing in the unseen Christ, than Thomas had for believing in the seen Christ.

The first advantage we have over Thomas is, we do not confuse the Christ, the very incarnate Son of God, with the Galilean carpenter. This Thomas did. People are prone to form wrong opinions of all men if they view them from too close a range. People were continually asking the question, "Is this not the carpenter of Nazareth?" It was hard for them to see how God could be a Galilean carpenter. It is impossible for us to get a proper perspective of a building if we are within a few inches of it. We must be some distance from the building if we would see it in its entirety. So, for us to have a perfect view of Jesus as the son of god, we must see him from the viewpoint of a later day than the one in which he lived. Our savior realized this truth when he said, "It is expedient for you that I go away. You need to be led into all truth, and this cannot be until the Spirit of Truth has come. He will make you see some of the mysteries of my Godship, which you cannot see if I remain here in the flesh." This was the thought of Jesus.. We do to know how Jesus looked physically, and like the burial place of Moses, God has kept this information from us for a reason. He does not want us to be more concerned, as were some of the early disciples, with the physical Jesus, than we are with the Son of God.

Again, we have the advantage of seeing the very event that Thomas doubted as one of the best proved occurrences in history. I was talking with a Unitarian minister a few years ago, who, at the time, was getting ready an Easter service to be held in his church. When I expressed surprise that he should be preparing to observe Easter, he said to me, "Why, the Bible is right when it says we have many infallible proofs of his resurrection." Now this was the very thing Thomas was doubting. He had never been disciplined in believing what to him seemed unreasonable. Were he living today there would be no place in such a sincere life for such doubt.

Furthermore, we have written documents of the New Testament that Thomas did not have. He had never read closely the Sermon on the Mount. He had heard it, but hearing is one thing, and reading and meditating on it is quite another. He had not the advantage of reading this very text and passage, founded on his mistake, and given to us for our edification, that we may not make the same mistake.

We also have two thousand years of history with Christian principles as they have been infused into the home life, the political life, and the social life of nations. This furnishes many infallible proofs. In the days of Thomas, no orphan homes, no hospitals, no nurses, no doctors, no sanitary laws, no religious freedom had grown our of Christian civilization. He had associated with but few Christians, for there were but few as yet with whom to associate. He had never attended a great convention and looked at thousands from many nations earnestly sing, "All Hail the Power of Jesus Name." Pentecost as yet had not confirmed his faith. We have all these things to confirm our faith. These things are here, because Jesus went home to the Father.

****

After seeing our ground for such belief in the unseen Christ, let us emphasize the importance of exercising such faith. The New Testament tells us, "Without faith it is impossible to please God." The passage might have added, it is impossible to please man without faith. Some one has said that Jesus marveled twice, once at the unbelief of men, and once at a man's faith. "Blessed are the persons who believe in the unseen Christ," according to Jesus. If they are blessed, then they are happy; if happy, then this happiness is a result of faith in the unseen Christ. Doubt is the creator of fear, and fear makes men miserable.

This faith in the unseen Christ is the one thing good men have had in common in all ages. Moses, Abraham, Isaiah, Amos, Paul, Spurgeon, Beecher, Moody, and all others have thus seen the invisible Christ, who belong to the company of the blest.

Jesus thought this faith in him of sufficient importance to make the lack of it a ground of condemnation. He said we were condemned already if we have not believed on him. Not to believe in Jesus is the greatest sin in the catalog of sins.

Faith, from the religious viewpoint, is exercising trust in the unseen Savior. The object of faith is the most important thing connected with it. Our faith is in Jesus, and he is sufficient. A drowning man may catch at a straw with a great faith. This, however, does not keep him from strangling in the water. A little faith in a great God is of much more value than a big faith in nothing. A woman was asked if she was the person who had such a great faith, and her answer is thought provoking, " No, I have but little faith, but this faith is in a great God."

    You cannot start the Christian life without faith; you cannot continue in it without faith. You cannot overcome temptations without faith. This is the victory that overcomes the world, even our faith.

An Overlooked Beatitude.

Remember the words of the Lord Jesus, how he said, It is more blessed to give than to receive (Acts 20:35).

Chapter XVII.

The Beatific Verity On Liberality.

In boyhood days I have stood the banks of overflowing streams in the high water seasons of spring and early summer, and many a time I have watched the muddy water murmur their ways to their destinations. Sometimes a valuable piece of property would come floating down, which the boatmen, from the banks of the angry stream, would go and make haste to rescue, before it was destroyed.

Matther, Mark, and Luke have given us what we call the synoptic Gospels. They report the sayings of our Savior to us. John gives us the supplemental gospel in which he aims to add something to what the others have said. Especially is his a supplement to Luke's Gospel. When John finished his book in which he had recalled many things of our Christ, which the others had left unsaid, he saw a great many things still unused. Then he made the statement, if all Christ said were written, the world would not contain the books. How we long to know the things he said but were never recorded! Paul helps us out a little in giving us our text. Matthew Mark, Luke, and John all leave it unused. Paul quotes it for us in such a way that we know it was known by the Christians at that time. "For remember the words of the Lord Jesus." Evidently these words were known, for we generally remember only the things we already know. Paul seems to rush out into the destroying stream of time and rescue to our good, this one more saying of Jesus; this saying well known, but evidently over-looked by the others.

Now this overlooked beatitude is a very familiar passage, and is treated as the other beatitudes, quoted much, preached from very little, and believed and practiced very seldom. You hardly ever read sermons from this text, and yet every Sunday school student in the land can quote it glibly. Like most passages which are much quoted and seldom preached from, it has been twisted to mean many things our Savior never meant it to mean. Like the other beatitudes, it is paradoxical, using terms which are opposites, such as "receiving" and "giving". Like the others, it contradicts the existing standards and conceptions of the age. For that matter, it contradicts standards as they are held by some people even today. The religions of the time, and the moral systems of other lands, reverse this statement in their ideas. The Pharisees do not think it more blessed to give than to receive, but spend all their time trying to get something more to add to their characters and records. So with many other systems that try to work out their salvation. They do not realize that the statement is true, "Character is the fine art of giving up," and that to be saved is to surrender, or give over, and not to work for something and add it to your life.

Many who do not study this passage closely, make receiving a sin, and giving a virtue, over against it. This is wrong. They are a part of the same thing, and both have their place. Receiving is a rare privilege, indeed, and we should be very poor if we never passed through this experience. But receiving is a blessing only when it leads to something else, bigger and better. It is a blessing when it is a means toward an end. It is a decided curse, when it becomes an end in itself. There is nothing in the world that makes us a recipient, except with the expectation of our becoming a giver. The Government of our great Nation makes us to receive many things. We receive liberty, right to hold property, right to protect homes, right to worship God as we please. All of this is given, but with the full understanding that we contribute our part in taxes, suffrage, and, if need be, life, to the good of the state. We receive that we may give. The giving is the last and the greatest thing connected with the whole process. We might carry the thought into the realm of learning. We receive first, before we can give, second, in matters of scholarship and knowledge. All the schooling we receive, whether we get it from the grades or the universities, is given us that we may be able to contribute to the general educational world about us. The state does not educate, nor do the denominations, simply to satisfy a thirst for knowledge. This is all done to put us in a position to serve humanity.

Receiving is not a sin, but is is not the greatest and final good thing connected with our lives. Receiving is but a John the Baptist blazing a way through the forest for something bigger and better to follow. It is but the springtime, and, as such, simply prepares the way for the coming summer or giving. The means is never as important as the end for which the means came into being

It is true because the giving out follows more of God's example and, of course, has more of his approval than receiving. Christ came not to be ministered unto but to minister and give his life a ransom for many. He in a way received much. Many gave of their possessions to his comfort. His mother took care of him, and he was entertained in the homes of his friends while here. He did receive, but he always considered the receiving a means to an end, and the fundamental principle of his life was "not to be served, but to serve."

There is a much-used story of a priest who thought to get near to God. He climbed into the steeple of his church and there prayed constantly to be near to God and to be like him in character. One day while he was praying, a voice came to him, "Go down where the people are." What was the reason for this voice? "It is more blessed to give than to receive."

The giving part of life is a more blessed experience than the receiving part, because it is more helpful to humanity. Anything that helps humanity blesses the possessor of such a thing. No matter what a person receives, he is a blessing to humanity with it only when he gives it and uses it to their good. We get, to give. The old time water mills were never turned by the streams receiving water, but by the streams giving away the water they had already received. Receiving water never made any enclosure grow a lily, irrigate a meadow, water a bird or beast. It is the giving that blesses,. And as it blesses, it ceased to become a Dead-Sea affair, and keeps sweet and pure. All the good things a bountiful Father has given you can be added to by you, and made sweeter by you, if you will but contribute of them to others.

It is more blessed to give than to receive, because the giving makes us interested in anything, while the receiving will not. To receive requires no effort. It is a passive exercise, and such never created an interest in anything. This is cleverly brought out in the history of Israel. When they sacrificed cattle and sheep, it was not to please God. As far as God was concerned, he would have preferred to see these animals eating grass on a thousand hills. But God knew human nature enough to know that if Israel was to be kept interested in religion, that religion must be an expensive thing to her. He know that it is more blessed to give than it is to receive.

Again, if Israel had simply taken the good things of God, eaten the manna and quails, she would have remained an illiterate and helpless race of slaves forever. God made Israel a nation by making her give. This is an universally true principle. A race horse is fed to make muscle and, in the end, produce speed. The hog is fed to make fat. The muscle is made not only by the receiving, but by an added and higher process that of giving. Eating food never grew a strong muscle. Reading books never made an educated man. Unassimilated ideas, like undigested food, are a detriment, instead of a help. Men learn to swim by giving, not receiving. People develop in the Christian life by giving; never by receiving.

Our text tells us that it is a more blessed thing to give than it is to receive. To have a blessed experience is to have a happy experience. It is a most unhappy thing to be a Dead-Sea Christian. It is a happy thing to be a Jordan-River Christian. The only way for us to enjoy our religious privileges and opportunities, is to be constant givers of what we have received.

The Touchstone Of Destiny.

And blessed is he, whosoever shall not be offended in me (Matt. 11:6)

And he beheld them, and said, What is this then that is written, The stone which the builders rejected, the same is become the head of the corner? Whosoever shall fall on that stone shall be broken: but on whomsoever it shall fall, it will grind him to powder (Luke 20:17, 18).

Chapter XVIII

The Beatific Verity On Not Being Offended In Christ.

After all the changes of time have come and this civilization, like others before it, has thrown away many things of an unabiding nature, there will be a lasting thing as expressed in our texts. The relation which you sustain to Christ will always determine your usefulness and happiness here, as well as your destiny hereafter. He is, indeed, the touchstone of destiny.

These texts are taken from different places in the New Testament, and from different times in our Savior's public ministry; but they carry home to our hearts much of the same lessons. The word we translate, "offended,," means to find an occasion of stumbling. A person is offended in any one when he stumbles because of that one. This first passage then would read, "Blessed is he who does not find an occasion of stumbling in me." The second adds an idea when it says such a person will be broken to pieces by such a stumbling over Jesus. Then it gives an added idea, that the stone of stumbling will not always remain passive, but it shall some day become active and grind to powder all who are offended. They both clearly bring out that thought that the relation you sustain to Jesus is that which determines happiness here and hereafter. It will always be so.

By studying these passages closely we can see possible reasons for people being offended in Jesus. The first reason we might assign is for one to be placed in an environment to which he is unaccustomed and given an atmosphere he is not used to breathing. John the Baptist was in a dungeon, and he was accustomed to breathe only the mountain air. This damp air of the dungeon, and the dark room of his place of confinement, caused him to question the Christ he was trying to serve. It was like placing a red bird in a canary's cage. The only thing it does under such circumstances is to beat its wings against the wires until they bleed.

Elijah, Peter, and Luther are good men of the past who have had dispositions similar to that of John the Baptist. They were susceptible to environment. The wrong environment nearly always caused them to become despondent and to doubt God's love and the final outcome of goodness. It does not take a very close observer today to see that many are offended in Jesus because of an environment which is not helpful to Christian activity and which is not an encouragement to Christian living.

Again we can see that to take a short-sighted view of reverses and adversity, will quite often cause one to be offended in Jesus. Why John was in prison he did not know. He wondered about it, and never thought that,

> "Sweet are the uses of adversity.
> Which, like a toad, ugly and venomous,
> Wears yet a jewel in its head."

Again, misunderstood delay will sometimes cause doubt and questioning. John no doubt entertained a notion that some time Jesus would rescue him from the prison cell. But instead, he was left there. The help he expected did not come. Quite often Christian workers have met people who, when in distress, trusted Christ for a while, but thinking he was not going to come to them, gave up in despair. They continually ask the question, "Why does

God let me suffer?" That is a question we cannot answer, and yet it is a perplexing one to many.

Again, he was very much disappointed with the history of Christ's work. He had said, "He shall put the ax to the root of the tree. His fan is in his hand." He expected a violent Christ, one who should rule by force. From John's day, including him, men have tried to take the kingdom by force. He expected a different kind of a leader and Messiah. The word, "hetheron," used in the sentence, "shall we look for another?" means, shall we look for a different kind? Shall we look for a "hetheron" leader? Christ's methods were decidedly different from what John expected and said about them. The way Jesus was doing, was enough to make John appear inconsistent to the world. History is being made today at a rapid pace. A thousand years are sometimes crowded into a day. Many are looking out upon the unfolding things of history and are being offended in Christ. Christianity is being blamed for things as they are happening in Europe. While some are manifesting disappointment that there was not enough love of
God in the world to prevent the war, others are busy telling us that God is sanctioning it, because he sanctioned war in the past. Now the truth about the whole affair is this: God did not cause the war, nor did he want it, nor does he sanction it. Furthermore, he never has sanctioned bloodshed. The leaders in some of the past ages said god told them to kill and cause bloodshed, just like leaders are imagining god wants them to turn themselves into butchers today. Unfolding history causes much offense in God, and many to stumble, but God is not responsible for such.

John was a wise man in one thing at least. He knew where to go when he was offended. He took it directly to

Jesus, and the reasons were all given and the misunderstanding all cleared up.

It is a most blessed thing for people not to be offended in Jesus. The offended one is the sufferer. Now Jesus does not want anybody to be ashamed of him, and to stumble because of him; but when they do such things, they are the persons who suffer most from the fall. When people turn their backs on Christ because they do not understand the providences of God, they sometimes imagine God and Christ and the churches will be hurt. In a way all suffer, for Christian sympathy makes all Christians want the cause to prosper and the people to do right; but by far the greatest sufferer is the offended one.

Jesus Christ is the touchstone of destiny. If you turn your back on him and his message, you have sealed your own future forever. He is to you what the shepherd is to the sheep, the vine to the branch, and the ark of the covenant to Israel, the lamp to Aladdin. The stone which the builders rejected was the one stone needed in the building of the temple. So to stumble over Christ is to be broken to pieces.

Paul said, "I can do all things through Christ which strengtheneth me." This Christ was to him strength and help. After the battle of Marango, Napoleon had some medals struck for his soldiers. On one side of the medal was the name and date of the battle, and on the other, these words: "I was there." Of course, he desired to give the thought that his being there was the cause of the victory.

As a Roman ship sailed the sea, a storm came up and the passengers were very much frightened. At last it came to be known that the emperor was a passenger. Then the word went around, "Be not afraid, the emperor is on this ship."

Jesus said unto his disciples in the early days. "Be not afraid, it is I." He that spared not his own son, will surely with him freely give us all things. He is the key to the whole problem of life. He is the touchstone of human destiny.

God's Burials
And I heard a voice from heaven saying unto me, Write, Blessed are the dead which die in the Lord from henceforth: Yea, saith the Spirit, that they may rest from their labors; and their works do follow them (Rev. 14:13)

Chapter XIX

The Beatific Verity On The Dead In The Lord.

Any system of religious truth making a successful appeal to the race of men, as it works out its destiny here, must give a definite and final message about the noble dead. This is true because of the universality of graveyards. Nations may differ in many things, but they are alike in this – all have given up their loved ones. Even homes are alike in this one thing, for we find a vacant chair in nearly every home. Then we also see, not only a universal custom of giving up loved ones, but a casual observer cannot help but note that we always give them up with some sort of hope. Of course, in many places this hope is very crudely expressed, but it always finds enough expression to make us know the hope exists. These two things make it necessary for the religion that hopes for a universal response, and that claims to be the final religion, to speak a word on this subject.

In answer to these hopes, Christ presents another Beatific Verity. It is given an expression thus: "And I heard a voice from heaven saying unto me, Write, Blessed are the dead which die in the Lord from henceforth: Yea, saith the Spirit, that they may rest from their labors; and their works do follow them." Rev.14:13.

In this passage there are two seeming contradictions expressed. Public opinion is opposed in two places, and these things are not made mention of by accident. The one is the paradox expressed in the words, "Happy, or blessed, are the dead." This ideal of death has never been associated with the idea of happiness. Not even the systems of religious truth did this. It was always thought of with gloom and sadness. Of course, we expect that in the heathen religions, but to our surprise we see it also in the Jewish religious thought. Their Sheol was not a place to be longed for. No active person would have a special desire to go there. It might be sought by persons tormented with afflictions and troubles, but never by a well, prosperous person. When our loved ones leave we often say, "I would not call them back," but such a word the old Jew would not have spoken. Since Jesus lived, many who do not follow him associate the idea of death with that of gloom. One monarch said, "Never mention death in my presence, on penalty of death." So, realizing the thoughts of the world unto death, we can see what a contradictory thought was presented by the text.

Another paradox as expressed here, is the fact that the dead in the Lord shall rest from their labors, but at the same time their works shall follow them. How can they rest with working? This of course contradicts popular notions.

Now I think one of these expressions gives meaning and significance to the other. They shall have an active rest, and this will insure their state of blessedness. The Christian's heaven is a place of completion of many things. The lack of completion gives earth its sorrow and pain. But the fullness of all things in heaven gives it its glory.

Our knowledge is to be crowned in this country toward which we travel. It is the continuing to learn that makes one with a passion for knowledge long to be there. Our ignorance is surprising.

When we think of the world around us, existing by our side, how forcefully this truth comes home to us. Men of inquiring minds have divided the subject of the natural universe into different realms, and then subdivided over and over again, in this way hoping to cover the ground. But we cannot as a race tell all that God knows about the smallest flower.

> *"Flower in the crannied wall,*
> *I pluck you out of crannies;*
> *Hold you here, root and all, in my hand,*
> *Little flower; but if I could understand*
> *What you are, root and all, and all in all,*
> *I should know what God and man is."*

Men who bury themselves and work for years to understand a few of nature's secrets may some day know as they are known. A good God will not repay them for their labor with giving them no opportunity of ever knowing.

We know but little about ourselves. This knowledge is also longed for. Over the arches of the Greek temples were the oft-quoted words, "Know thyself." But who has heeded the admonition? To know what one person is in all his faculties, one must know all the past of the race, all the present of it, and all the future of it. Now it is a fact that we know comparatively little about the past. Authentic history reaches back but a few years. The race, from all we can learn, reaches back for millenniums. We do not know a great deal about the present. We have no knowledge at all of the future. Since our knowledge is limited in all these realms, then we know but little about the human race. But are we never to know? Yes, some day, according to Christian teaching, we are to know. How? By dying. The grain of wheat may know its wrapped-up possibilities in only one way, and that way is not by "fruitless conservation, but prolific decay." So it is with us. The only way the boy can have the longed-for knowledge of a man, is to have the boy killed, and the man to come from the death of the boy. "When I became a man, I put away childish things." The only way we may have full hoped-for knowledge of humanity in all its possibilities, is to be of the blessed dead.

We long for knowledge of God. In all ages men have sought to find out God. They have looked for him in the stars; they have listened for his voice in the sighing of the winds; they have looked for his face in the storm cloud and lightning; but have they found him? Not completely. We know but little here below, nor know that little long, as far as God is concerned. Shall we ever know? The Christian message says we may. As Wm. Blake lay dying, he said, "I am soon to be going to that country that I have always longed to see." Charles Kingsley said, "God forgive me, but I face the future with a reverent curiosity." Ian Maclaren adds, "He needed not to ask for forgiveness for this." Paul thinks to be with Christ is far better than any earthly company.

> *"Some day the silver cord will break,*
> *And I no more as now shall sing;*
> *But O, the joy, when I shall wake*
> *Within the palace of the King."*

We also see that the noble dead shall be blessed in that they shall find a completion to life's achievements. No man who is interested in his work finds enough time or enough equipment, or congenial enough company, to carry it to completion. But few workmen can say, "It is finished." What little work they do is done with weariness, and to wear out is the certain end of energetic workers in all realms.

Michael Angelo sometimes slept with his clothes on that he might get up at any time and do more work. He worked till he was an old man, and then lamented the fact that he had not finished his task. Handel secretly practiced his music in the attic, and Bach copied whole studies by moonlight, being deprived of candles by an unsympathetic brother. Lincoln worked his problems on a pine board by the light of an open fireplace. West is compelled to get bristles for his paint brushes from the back of the family cat. Joshua Reynolds worked from sun till sun, and then sometimes almost wept because it was time to go to bed. It is said that Dryden accomplished the work of ten men, and thought his labor was unfinished. Mozart said, "Work is my chief pleasure." When Chalmers, after a visit to London, was asked what Foster was doing, he replied, "Hard at it at the rate of a line a week." Adam Smith died regretting that he had done so little. The great memorial of Sir Walter Scott in Edinburgh stands as a tribute to a great man, but he is said to have taken his own life, because of dissatisfaction with his task. After Lyman Beecher had preached his greatest sermon, "The Government of God," and was asked as he descended the pulpit stairs, how long it took him to prepare it, answered, "About forty years, sir." Victor Hugo says, "When I go down to the grave I must say like so many others, 'I have finished my day's work.' But I cannot say, 'I have finished my life.' My day's work will begin the next morning. The tomb is not a blind alley. It is a thoroughfare. It closes in the twilight to open in the dawn." Robert Louis Stevenson gave voice to a sentence that expressed the thought of every man who loves his work of whatever line, "I leave my work with a ragged edge, for sunset comes too soon."

So in earthly achievements of whatever nature, even of the greatest, we see weariness, incompleteness, lack of time, lack of equipment. Will it ever be thus? No, in the Christian's heaven there will be work without weariness; we shall rest by the working. Thousands will be glad that we shall have an opportunity to finish what we have begun. Kipling's idea of heaven is doing what you want to do, as you want to do it, and with as much time and equipment as you need.

"When earth's last picture is painted, and the tubes are all twisted and dried,
When the oldest colors are faded and the youngest critic has died,
We shall rest – and, faith, we shall need it – lie down for an eon or two,
'Till the Master of All Good Workmen shall set us to work anew.
"All those who were good shall be happy: they shall sit in a golden chair;
They shall splash at a ten-league canvas, with brushes of comet's hair;
They shall find real saints to draw from – Magdalene, Peter and Paul;
They shall work for an age at a sitting, and never grow weary at all.
"And only the Master shall praise us, and only the Master shall blame;
And no one shall work for money, and no one shall work for fame;
But each for the joy of working, and each in his separate star,

Shall draw the thing as he sees it, for the God of things as they are."

The noble dead shall be blessed in that they shall find completion to life's associations with their friendships and loves. The happiest conditions of this life are the ones where we find friendship and love expressed, and where there are pleasant and congenial associations. God gave the human being a gregarious instinct, but it goes without saying that this tendency is only partially lived out here. Will it ever be followed in completion? I think so. Tennyson shall meet his Hallam, Poe shall see his lost Lenore. Earthly love, as beautiful as it is is quite incomplete.

It cannot mean the most to us here because of our misunderstandings of each other. It takes understanding in perfection to bring perfect love.

> *"If I knew you and you knew me,*
> *And both of us could clearly see,*
> *And with an inner light, divine*
> *The meaning of your heart and mine,*
> *I'm sure that we would differ less,*
> *And clasp our hands in friendliness.*
> *Our thoughts would mutually agree,*
> *If I knew you and you knew me."*

But this knowledge will never come here within this mundane sphere.

Furthermore, we have not the time to love as we ought. Just as we learn to love and appreciate, then parting comes with its heartaches and weeping. A little girl was walking with her father under a starry sky, and as she looked into the beautiful blue of God's heaven, was heard to say, "Papa, if the wrong side of heaven is so beautiful, what must the right side be?" Only a childish thought of heaven above the skies, but at the same time you can see the force of the illustration. If love on earth is so dear, "What must it be to be there?"

Again, in the eternal realms, according to the Christian word on this subject, we shall see the crowning of character. That is the end of all good works on earth; character of the proper type. God's making the earth, beautifying it, inhabiting it, lighting it, watering it, feeding; God's redemptive love expressed in his Son, living, dying, coming from the grave, ascending to heaven – all these things were for the purpose of making Christian character. But it is very incomplete here. We pray, study the Bible, do Christian work, and then say as we pass out, "Must I go empty handed?" We say then, "Saved by grace." Is it always to be thus? I think not.

There it shall receive its crown, and there will we know what Christian character really means. I cannot tell you the difference between the body Jesus had before his resurrection, and the one he had afterward. Some others who think they can tell, would know more if they did not know so many things that are not so. But I do know that one was subject to fatigue and space limitations. He was weary with a journey and sat down on a well to rest. The other evidently was not thus limited, for he appeared as if by magic to the disciples on the road to Emmaus, and went through closed doors. Now, he is the first fruits of them that slept, and limitations as we have them shall be removed. Our characters will have ample room and ample opportunities of expression. On the tomb of Dr. Condor in London are these words: "I have sinned, repented, loved, I rest, and I shall rise and reign." On the tomb of Moody in Northfield, we read the following words: "He who doeth the will of the Lord abideth forever." Then men who are just here shall be made perfect there. This is the Christian's message.

But what is the key to this blessedness as given in our message? To be found "in the Lord." "Blessed are the dead that die in the Lord." And if
we be there, then the tides of providence will only ebb and flow to our profit forever and forever.

www.ingramcontent.com/pod-product-compliance
Lightning Source LLC
Chambersburg PA
CBHW061657040426
42446CB00010B/1782